Workshop on Modeling Large Scale Social Interaction in Massively Open Online Courses 2014

Held at the Conference on Empirical Methods in Natural Language Processing (EMNLP 2014)

Doha, Qatar
25 October 2014

ISBN: 978-1-63439-483-3

Printed from e-media with permission by:

Curran Associates, Inc.
57 Morehouse Lane
Red Hook, NY 12571

Some format issues inherent in the e-media version may also appear in this print version.

Printed by Curran Associates, Inc. (2014)

For permission requests, please contact the Association for Computational Linguistics at the address below.

Association for Computational Linguistics
209 N. Eighth Street
Stroudsburg, Pennsylvania 18360

Phone: 1-570-476-8006
Fax: 1-570-476-0860

acl@aclweb.org

Additional copies of this publication are available from:

Curran Associates, Inc.
57 Morehouse Lane
Red Hook, NY 12571 USA
Phone: 845-758-0400
Fax: 845-758-2634
Email: curran@proceedings.com
Web: www.proceedings.com

Introduction

Welcome to the EMNLP 2014 Workshop on Modeling Large Scale Social Interaction in Massively Open Online Courses. An emerging area for real world impact of technology for analysis of social media at a large scale is online education in Massively Open Online Courses (MOOCs). The goal of this workshop is to explore what the language technologies community has to offer this endeavor. At this one day workshop organized around a shared task related to analysis of large scale social interaction in MOOCs, we will grapple with the competing images of the inner workings of massive learning communities provided by alternative computational approaches.

With the recent press given to online education and increasing enrollment in online courses, the need for scaling up quality educational experiences online has never been so urgent. Current offerings provide excellent materials including video lectures, exercises, and some forms of discussion opportunities. One important hurdle that prevents MOOCs from reaching their transformative potential is that they fail to provide the kind of social environment that is conducive to sustained engagement and learning, especially as students arrive in waves to these online learning communities. While limited, current affordances for social interaction in MOOCs have already shown some value for providing students with connection to others that provides some needed motivational benefits.

Computational modeling of massive scale social interaction has the potential to yield new knowledge about the inner-workings of interaction in such environments so that support for healthy community formation can be designed and built. However, the state-of-the-art in graphical models applied to large scale social data provides representations of the data that are challenging to interpret in light of specific questions that may be asked from a learning sciences or social psychological perspective. What is needed are new methodologies for development and interpretation of models that bridge expertise from machine learning and language technologies on one side and learning sciences, sociolinguistics, and social psychology on the other side. The field of language technologies has the human capital to take leadership in making these breakthroughs. Other specific opportunities for the field associated with that enterprise are problems in assessment of student work (e.g., automated essay scoring), generation of in process feedback for students learning online independently or in groups (e.g. tutorial dialogue agents), support for large scale threaded discussions (e.g., dialogue agent based facilitation), and summarization of participation data for facilitators and course developers who revise and maintain course materials (e.g., conversation summarization).

MOOCs are especially interesting as a source of large scale social data. The unique developmental history of MOOCs creates challenges that require insight into the inner-workings of massive scale social interaction in order to meet. In particular, rather than evolving gradually as better understood forms of online communities, MOOCs spring up overnight and then expand in waves as new cohorts of students arrive from week to week to begin the course. As massive communities of strangers that lack shared practices that would enable them to form supportive bonds of interaction, these communities grow in an unruly manner. While some students may successfully find birds of a feather with whom to bond and find support, when others come they may find an overwhelming amount of communication having already been posted that they feel lost in. Others may find themselves somewhere in between these two extremes. They may begin to form weak bonds with some other students when they join, however, massive attrition may create challenges as members who have begun to form bonds with fellow students soon find their virtual cohort dwindling. Early attempts to organize the community into smaller study groups may be thwarted by such periodic growth spurts paired with attrition, as groups that initially had an appropriate critical mass soon fall below that level and then are unable to support the needs of remaining students. Can our models serve as useful lenses to offer insights into these social processes? Come to the workshop and join in the discussion!!

Organizers:

Carolyn Rosé, Carnegie Mellon University

George Siemens, University of Texas at Arlington

Program Committee

Hua Ai, Georgia Institute of Technology

Ryan Baker, Teacher's College, Columbia University

Kristy Boyer, North Carolina State University

Emma Brunskill, Carnegie Mellon University

Brian Butler, University of Maryland

Hal Daumé III, University of Maryland

Barbara Di Eugenio, University of Illinois at Chicago

Jana Diesner, University of Illinois at Urbana-Champaign

Jacon Eisenstein, Georgia Institute of Technology

Dragan Gasevic, Athabasca University

Neil Heffernan, Worcester Polytechnic

Eduard Hovy, Carnegie Mellon University

Lillian Lee, Cornell University

Alice Oh, Korea Advanced Institute of Science and Technology

Mari Ostendorf, University of Washington

Keith Sawyer, University of North Carolina

Hinrich Schuetze, University of Munich

Simon Buckingham Shum, The Open University

Yla Tausczik, Carnegie Mellon University

Stephanie Teasley, University of Michigan

Joel Tetreault, Nuance

Chong Wang, Carnegie Mellon University

Jason Williams, Microsoft Research

Alyssa Wise, Simon Fraser University

Eric Xing, Carnegie Mellon University

Table of Contents

Conference Program

Saturday, October 25, 2014

Session 1

09:00–09:20 *Opening Remarks*
The organizers

09:20–10:30 *Keynote: Data Archeology: A theory informed approach to analyzing data traces of social interaction in large scale learning environments*
Alyssa Wise

10:30–10:50 ***Coffee Break***

Session 2

10:50–11:15 *Your click decides your fate: Inferring Information Processing and Attrition Behavior from MOOC Video Clickstream Interactions*
Tanmay Sinha, Patrick Jermann, Nan Li and Pierre Dillenbourg

11:15–11:40 *Identifying Student Leaders from MOOC Discussion Forums through Language Influence*
Seungwhan Moon, Saloni Potdar and Lara Martin

11:40–12:05 *Towards Identifying the Resolvability of Threads in MOOCs*
Diyi Yang, Miaomiao Wen and Carolyn Rose

12:05–12:30 *Point-of-View Mining and Cognitive Presence in MOOCs: A (Computational) Linguistics Perspective*
Noureddine Elouazizi

12:30–14:00 ***Lunch***

Saturday, October 25, 2014 (continued)

Session 3

15:30–16:00 ***Coffe Break***

Session 4

Keynote: Data Archeology: A Theory Informed Approach to Analyzing Data Traces of Social Interaction in Large Scale Learning Environments

Alyssa Friend Wise
Faculty of Education
Simon Fraser University
250-13450 102 Avenue
Surrey BC, Canada, V3T 0A3
alyssa_wise@sfu.ca

Abstract

Data archeology is a theoretically-informed approach to make sense of the digital artifacts left behind by a prior learning "civilization." Critical elements include use of theoretical learning models to construct analytic metrics, attention to temporality as a means to reconstruct individual and collective trajectories, and consideration of the pedagogical and technological structures framing activity. Examples of the approach using discussion forum trace data will be presented.

1 Overview

Data traces that learners leave in online systems offer the possibility to study learning activity, predict outcomes, and designed targeted interventions for support (Siemens & Long, 2011). However, such analysis often focus on rudimentary learning *processes* (series of related actions engaged in as part of learning activities) without attention to the larger learning *practices* they make up (repertoires of processes organized around particular foci that have meaning recognized within a particular context and social group) [Arastoopour et al., 2014]. This is an important concern for all learning analytics, but particularly problematic when the desired target of analytic claims is social interactions.

Lockyer, Heathcote & Dawson (2013) conceptualize this issue through the relationship between learning analytics and learning design. That is, creation and interpretation of valid analytic measures needs to be grounded in the "the pedagogical and technical context in which the data [was] generated" (p. 1440). The practical implications of such are that the same analytic measures and patterns in these measures may be more or less useful, valid, and valued depending on the pedagogical goals of the activity at a particular point in time. For example, a discussion forum may be used in an online course course as a place for Q &A with experts (or relatively expert-peers) or for common interest groups to work through different ways the course material might apply to a particular situation or challenge. A social network analysis of discussion replies that produces a wheel-and-spoke structure may be appropriate (and desired) for the former situation, but problematic in the latter (Brooks, Greer & Gutwin, 2014).

To address these issues I describe the notion of data archeology (Wise, 2013) as theoretically-informed efforts to make sense of the digital artifacts left behind by a prior "civilization." Critical aspects of taking a data archeology perspective include: (a) the use of theoretical models of learning to frame the construction and interpretation of analytic metrics; (b) attention to temporality (of data and analytic methods) as a means to reconstruct individual and collective trajectories of engagement and interaction; and (c) consideration of the pedagogical and technological structures framing the activity that occurred. Such an approach supports the development of rich indicators that instructors and learners can recognize as meaningful reflections of their particular practices of teaching and learning.

Examples of a data archeology approach to discussion forum traces will be presented grounding in the work of the E-Listening project (Wise et al., 2012; 2013; 2014a; 2014b), a research effort connecting the comments learners make in online discussions with actions in attending to the posts of others (invisible to other learners, but visible in the clickstream record). The conceptual categories of online listening

Proceedings of the 2014 Conference on Empirical Methods in Natural Language Processing (EMNLP), pages 1–2,
October 25-29, 2014, Doha, Qatar.

depth, breadth, integration and recursiveness will be introduced and their suitability for different kinds of technological and pedagogical discussion contexts discussed grounded in the framework of the following questions:

- What is the purpose of the educational activity taking place in the discussion forum?
- How does the design of the activity articulate with (support, inhibit) this purpose?
- What are expected (desired and undesirable) patterns of activity?
- How can these best be represented / proxied by the data available?

References

Arastoopour, G. et al. 2014. Analytics for Learning and Becoming in Practice. *Proceedings of the International Conference of the Learning Sciences, 2014,* 1680-1683.

Brooks, C., Greer, J. & Gutwin, C. 2014. The Data-Assisted Approach to Building Intelligent Technology Enhanced Learning Environments. In J. A. Larusson & B. White (Eds.) *Learning Analytics: From Research To Practice* (pp. 123-156). New York: Springer.

Lockyer, L., Heathcote, E., & Dawson, S. 2013. Informing Pedagogical Action: Aligning Learning Analytics with Learning Design. *American Behavioral Scientist,* 57(10): 1439-1459.

Siemens, G., & Long, P. 2011. Penetrating the Fog: Analytics in Learning And Education. *Educause Review*, 46(5): 30-32.

Wise, A. F. 2013. Moving Beyond (Mere) Narrative. (Invited Talk), In *Cyberinfrastructure for Design-Based Research Workshop,* Madison, WI.

Wise, A. F., Hausknecht, S. N. & Zhao, Y. 2014a. Attending to Others' Posts in Asynchronous Discussions: Learners' Online "Listening" and its Relationship to Speaking. *International Journal of Computer-Supported Collaborative Learning*, 9(2): 185-209.

Wise, A. F., Perera, N., Hsiao, Y., Speer, J. & Marbouti, F. 2012. Microanalytic Case Studies of Individual Participation Patterns in an Asynchronous Online Discussion in an Undergraduate Blended Course. *Internet and Higher Education,* 15(2): 108–117.

Wise, A. F., Speer, J., Marbouti, F. & Hsiao, Y. 2013. Broadening the Notion Of Participation in Online Discussions: Examining Patterns in Learners' Online Listening Behaviors. *Instructional Science.* 41(2): 323-343.

Wise, A. F., Zhao, Y. & Hausknecht, S. N. 2014b. Learning Analytics for Online Discussions: Embedded and Extracted Approaches. *Journal of Learning Analytics*, 1(2) : 48-71.

Your click decides your fate: Inferring Information Processing and Attrition Behavior from MOOC Video Clickstream Interactions

Tanmay Sinha[1], **Patrick Jermann**[2], **Nan Li**[3], **Pierre Dillenbourg**[3]
[1]Language Technologies Institute, Carnegie Mellon University, Pittsburgh PA 15213, USA
[2]Center for Digital Education, EPFL, CH 1015, Switzerland
[3]Computer-Human Interaction in Learning and Instruction, EPFL, CH 1015, Switzerland
[1]tanmays@andrew.cmu.edu, [2,3]<firstname.lastname>@epfl.ch

Abstract

In this work, we explore video lecture interaction in Massive Open Online Courses (MOOCs), which is central to student learning experience on these educational platforms. As a research contribution, we operationalize video lecture clickstreams of students into cognitively plausible higher level behaviors, and construct a quantitative information processing index, which can aid instructors to better understand MOOC hurdles and reason about unsatisfactory learning outcomes. Our results illustrate how such a metric inspired by cognitive psychology can help answer critical questions regarding students' engagement, their future click interactions and participation trajectories that lead to in-video & course dropouts. Implications for research and practice are discussed.

1 Introduction

Mushrooming as a scalable lifelong learning paradigm, Massive Open Online Courses (MOOCs) have enjoyed significant limelight in recent years, both in industry and academia (Haggard et al., 2013). The euphoria is about the transformative potential of MOOCs to revolutionize online education (North et al., 2014), by connecting and fostering interaction among millions of learners who otherwise would never have met and providing autonomy to these learners to grapple with the course instruction at their own pace of understanding. However, despite this expediency, there is also considerable skepticism in the learning analytics research community about MOOC productiveness (Nawrot and Antoine, 2014), primarily because of unsatisfactory learning outcomes that plague these educational platforms and induce a funnel of participation (Clow, 2013).

With a "one size fits all" approach that MOOCs follow, scaled up class sizes and lack of face to face interaction coupled with such high student teacher ratios (Guo and Katharina, 2014), students' motivation to follow the course oscillates (Davis et al., 2014). This is comprehensibly reflected in escalating attrition rates in MOOCs, ever since they have started maturing (Belanger and Thornton, 2013; Schmidt and Zach, 2013; Yang et al., 2013). Because it is not feasible for MOOC instructors to manually provide individualized attention that caters to different backgrounds, diverse skill levels, learning goals and preferences of students, there is an increasing need to make directed efforts towards automatically providing better personalized content in e-learning (Sinha et al., 2013; Lie et al., 2014; Sinha, 2014a). The provision of guidance with regard to the organization of the study and regulation of learning is a domain that also needs to be addressed.

A prerequisite for such an undertaking is that we, as MOOC researchers, understand how diverse ecologies of participation develop as students interact with the course material (Fischer, 2011), and how learners distribute their attention with multiple forms of computer mediated inputs in MOOCs. Learning in a MOOC requires that students apply self regulation. While substantial research has been done on studying MOOC discussion forums (Ramesh et al., 2013; Brinton et al., 2013; Anderson et al., 2014; Sinha, 2014b), grading strategies for assignments (Tillmann et al., 2013; Kulkarni et al., 2014) and deployment of reputation systems (Coetzee et al., 2014), inner workings of students' interaction while watching MOOC video lectures have been much less focused upon. Given that roughly 5% (Huang et al., 2014) of students actually participate in MOOC discussion forums, it would be legitimate to ask whether choosing video lectures as units of analysis would be more insightful. After 330,000 reg-

Proceedings of the 2014 Conference on Empirical Methods in Natural Language Processing (EMNLP), pages 3–14,
October 25-29, 2014, Doha, Qatar.

istrations in MOOC courses at EPFL in 2013, our experience reflects that out of the 100% students who register, 75% show up: 50% of them primarily watch video lectures and the rest 25% additionally work out homeworks and assignments. Thus, majority of students have video lecture viewing as their primary MOOC activity.

Video lectures form a primary and an extremely crucial part of MOOC instruction design. They serve as gateways to draw students into the course. Concept discussions, demos and tutorials that are held within these short video lectures, not only guide learners to complete course assignments, but also encourage them to discuss the taught syllabus on MOOC discussion forums. Specific to the context of video lectures, prior work has cut teeth on a)how video production style (slides, code, classroom, khan academy style etc) relates to students' engagement (Guo et al., 2014), b)what features of the video lecture and instruction delivery, such as slide transitions (change in visual content), instructor changing topic (topic modeling and ngram analysis) or variations in instructor's acoustic stream (volume, pitch, speaking rate), lead to peaks in viewership activity (Kim et al., 2014b). There has been increasing focus on unveiling numerous facets of complexity of raw click-level interactions resulting from student activities within individual MOOC videos (Kim et al., 2014a; Sinha et al., 2014). However, to the best of our knowledge, we present the first study that describes usage of such detailed clickstream information to form cognitive video watching states that summarize student clickstream. Instead of using summative features that express student engagement, we leverage recurring click behaviors of students interacting with MOOC video lectures, to construct their video watching profile.

Based on these richly logged interactions of students, we develop computational methods that answer critical questions such as a)how long will students grapple with the course material and what will their engagement trajectory look like, b)what future click interactions will characterize their behavior, c)whether students are ultimately going to survive through the end of the video and course. As an effort to improve the second generation of MOOC offerings, we perform a hierarchical three level clickstream analysis, rooted in foundations of cognitive psychology. Incidentally, we explore at a micro level whether, and how, cognitive mind states govern the formation and occurrence of micro level click patterns. Towards this end, we also develop a quantitative information processing index and monitor its variations among different student partitions that we define for the MOOC. Such an operationalization can help course instructors to reason how students' navigational style reflects cognitive resource allocation for meaning processing and retention of concepts taught in the MOOC. Our metric aids MOOC designers in identifying which part of the videos might require editing. The goal is to develop an explanatory techno-cognitive model which shows that a set of metrics derived from low-level behaviors are meaningful, and can in turn be used to make effective predictions on high-level behaviors intuitively.

In the remainder of this paper, we describe our study context in the next section. In section 3, we motivate our three level hierarchical MOOC video clickstream analysis (operations, actions, information processing activities), describing relevant related work along the way, along with the technical approach followed. In section 4, we validate our developed methodology by setting up certain machine learning experiments, specifically engagement prediction, next click state prediction, in-video and complete course dropout prediction. Implications for future work and conclusion is presented in section 5.

2 Study Context

The data for our current study comes from an introductory programming MOOC "Functional Programming in Scala" that was offered on the Coursera MOOC platform in 2012. This MOOC comprises 48 video lectures (10 Gb of JSON data), which has been parsed and preprocessed into a convenient format for experimentation. In these interaction logs, every click of students on the MOOC video player is registered (play, pause, seek forward, seek backward, scroll forward, scroll backward, ratechange). We have information about the rate at which the video lecture is played, total time spent on playing the video and time spent on/in-between various click events such as play, pause, seek etc. In total, 65969 students registered for the course, and 36536 of them had 762137 logged video interaction sessions containing the aforementioned types of click events. If a video is played till the end, then an automatic video-end pause is generated. Otherwise, the Coursera platform unfortunately does not log whether or not a student has left the video in the middle, leaving the true video engagement time unknown. To avoid biased data, we only include video sessions containing video-end pauses. This has yielded a dataset of 222021 video sessions from 21952 students for our analysis in this paper.

3 Operationalizing the Clickstream

3.1 Level 1 (Operations)

From our raw clickstream data, we construct a detailed encoding of students' clicks in the following 8 categories: Play (Pl), Pause (Pa), SeekFw (Sf), SeekBw (Sb), ScrollFw (SSf), ScrollBw (SSb), RatechangeFast (Rf), RatechangeSlow (Rs). When two seeks happen within a small time range ($<$ 1 sec), we group these seek events into a scroll. Additionally, to encode 'Rf' and 'Rs', we look for the playrate of the click event that occurs just before the 'Ratechange' click and compare it with students' currently changed playrate, to determine whether he has sped up/slowed down his playing speed. The reason behind encoding clickstreams to such specific categories, accommodating scrolling behavior and clicks representative of increase and decrease in video playing speed, is to experimentally analyze and understand the impact of such a granularity on our experiments, which are designed with an objective to capture the motley of differently motivated behavioral watching style in students.

As a next step, we concatenate these click events for every student, for every video lecture watched. Thus, the output from level 1 is this string of symbols that characterizes the sequence of clickstream events (video watching state sequence). For e.g: PlPaSfSfPaSbPa.., PlSSbPaRsRsPl..

3.2 Level 2 (Behavioral Actions)

Existing literature on web usage mining says that representing clicks using higher level categories, instead of raw clicks, better exposes the browsing pattern of users. This might be because high level categories have better noise tolerance than naive clickstream logs. The results obtained from grouping clickstream sequences at per click resolution are often difficult to interpret, as such a fine resolution leads to a wide variety of sequences, many of which are semantically equivalent. Therefore, to get more insights into student behavior in MOOCs, we group clicks encoded at very fine granularity into meaningful behavioral categories. Doing this also reduces sequence length which is easily interpretable. There is some existing literature (Banerjee and Ghosh, 2000; Wang et al., 2013), that just considers click as a binary event (yes/no) and discusses formation of concept based categories based on the area/sub area of the stimulus where the click was made.

To summarize a students' clickstream, we obtain n-grams with maximum frequency from the clickstream sequence (a contiguous sequence of 'n' click actions). Such a simple n-gram representation convincingly captures the most frequently occurring click actions that students make in conjunction with each other (n=4 was empirically determined as a good limit on clickstream subsequence overspecificity). Then, we construct seven semantically meaningful behavioral categories using these discovered n-grams, selecting representative click groups that occur within top 'k' most frequent n-grams (k=100). Each behavioral category acts like a latent variable, which is difficult to measure from data directly.

- **Rewatch**: PlPaSbPl, PlSbPaPl, PaSbPlSb, SbSbPaPl, SbPaPlPa, PaPlSbPa
- **Skipping**:SfSfSfSf, PaPlSfSf, PlSfSfSf, SfSfSfPa, SfSfPaPl, SfSfSfSSf, SfSfSSfSf, SfPaPlPa, PlPaPlSf
- **Fast Watching**: PaPlRfRf, RfPaPlPa, RfRfPaPl, RsPaPlRf, PlPaPlRf (click group of Ratechange fast clicks while playing or pausing video lecture content, indicating speeding up)
- **Slow Watching**: RsRsPaPl, RsPaPlPa, PaPlRsRs, PlPaPlRs, PaPlRsPa, PlRsPaPl (click group of Ratechange slow clicks while playing or pausing video lecture content, indicating slowing down)
- **Clear Concept**: PaSbPlSSb, SSbSbPaPl, PaPlSSbSb, PlSSbSbPa (a combination of SeekBw and ScrollBw clicks, indicating high tussle with the video lecture content)
- **Checkback Reference**: SbSbSbSb, PlSbSbSb, SbSbSbPa, SbSbSbSf, SfSbSbSb, SbPlSbSb, SSbSbSbSb (a wave of SeekBw clicks)
- **Playrate Transition**: RfRfRsRs, RfRfRfRs, RfRsRsRs, RsRsRsRf, RsRsRfRf, RfRfRfRf (a wave of ratechange clicks)

Case (Full, No, Partial match)	Clickstream A	Clickstream B	Fuzzy string matching verdict
1:Varying clickstream length	PlPa**PlSfPaSf**SbSbPl	PlPa**PlSfPaSf**SbSbPlPaSbSbSbRfRsRf (learner has performed lot more clicks)	Weight(P,A)>Weight(P,B)
2:Behavioral pattern appears more than once	PlPa**PlSfPaSf**SbSbPl	PlPa**PlSfPaSf**SbSbPl**PlSfPaSf** (pattern is more characteristic as it appears 2 times)	Weight(P,A)<Weight(P,B)
3:No appearance of behavioral pattern	RfSbSbRs	SSfSSfRsRsRsSfSfSfSfRfRfRfRfRf (string length doesn't matter)	Weight(P,A)≠(P,B) (very low weight)
4:Variation in number of individual clicks	RfSbSbRs**Pl**Sb**Pa**Sb	RfSbSbRs**Pl**Sb**SfPaSf**Sb (more clicks from pattern appear)	Weight(P,A)<Weight(P,B)
5:Variation in scattering of individual clicks	RfSbRs**Pl**Sb**SfPaSf**Sb (less scattering)	RfSbRs**Pl**SbSSb**Sf**PlSbRs**Pa**SbRf**Sf** (more scattering)	Weight(P,A)>Weight(P,B)
6:Reverse order of individual click appearance	RfRsSb**SfPaSf**Sb**Pl** (order reversed)	RfRs**Pl**Sb**SfPaSf**Sb (order maintained)	Weight(P,A)<Weight(P,B)

Table 1: Fuzzy string similarity weights for the sample behavioral action P("PlSfPaSf"). Weight(P, A/B) represents the similarity of the pattern P w.r.t clickstream sequence A or B.

In an attempt to quantify the importance of each of the above behavioral actions in characterizing the clickstream, we adopt a fuzzy string matching approach. Using this approach, we assign a weight to each of the grouped behavioral patterns for a given students' video watching state sequence (based on similarity of click groups present in each behavioral category, with the full clickstream sequence). The fuzzy string method (Van, 2014) is justified because it caters to the noise that might be present in raw clickstream logs of students, in six different ways, as mentioned in Table 1. After identifying these cases and meticulous experimental evaluation, we apply the following distance metrics and tuning parameters: Cosine similarity metric between the vector of counts of n-gram (n=4) occurrences for Cases 1 and 2, Levenshtein similarity metric for Cases 3 (weight for deletion=0, weight for insertion and substitution=1), 4, 5, 6 (weight for deletion=0.1, weight for insertion, substitution=1).

As a next step, all subcategories of click groups that lie within each behavioral category are aggregated by summing up the individual fuzzy string similarity weights that are obtained with respect to every students' clickstream sequence. Then, we perform a discretization of these summed up weights, for each behavioral category, by equal frequency (High/Low). The concern of adding up two distance metrics that do not lie in the same range, is thus alleviated, because the dichotomization automatically places highly negative values in the "Low" category and positive values closer to 0 in the "High" category. The result is a clickstream vector for each video viewing session of the student, where every element of the vector tells us about the weight (importance) of a behavioral category for characterizing the clickstream. Thus, the output from level 2 is such a summarized clickstream vector. For e.g: (Skipping=High, Fast Watching=High, Checkback Reference=Low, Rewatch=Low, ...).

3.3 Level 3 (Information Processing)

Watching MOOC videos is an interaction between the student and the medium, and therefore the conceptualization of higher-order thinking eventually leading to knowledge acquisition (Chi, 2000), is under control of both the a)student (who decides what video segment to watch, when and in what order to watch, how hard an effort be made to try and understand a specific video segment) and, b)medium/video lecture (the content or features of which decides what capacity allocation is required by the student to fully process the information contained).

Research has consistently found that the level of cognitive engagement is an important aspect of student participation (Carini et al., 2006). This cognitive processing is influenced by the appetitive (approach) and aversive (avoidance) motivational systems of a student, which activate in response to motivationally relevant stimuli in the environment (Cacioppo and Wendi, 1999). For example, in the context of MOOCs, the appetitive system's goal is in-depth exploration and information intake, while the aversive system primarily serves as a motivator for not attending to certain MOOC video segments. Thus, click behaviors representative of appetitive motivational system are rewatch/clear concept/slow watching, while click behaviors representative of aversive motiva-

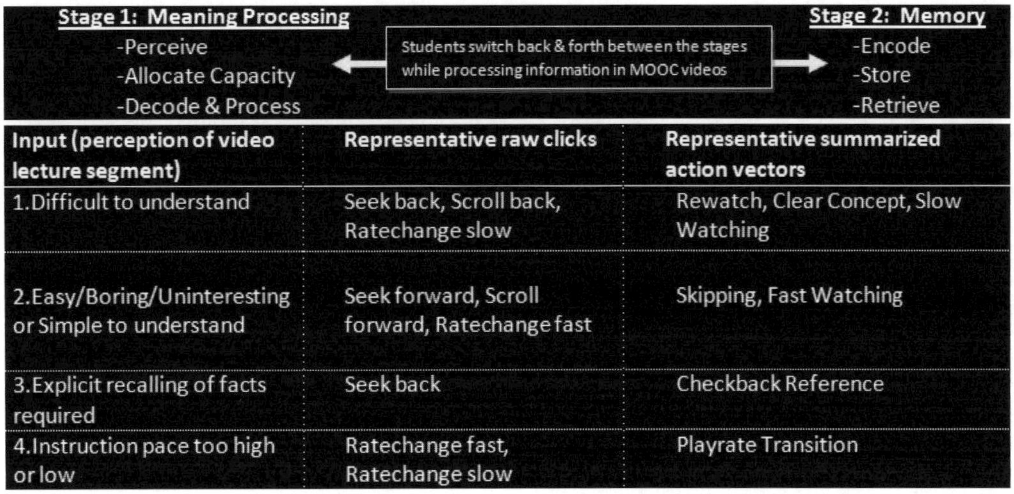

Figure 1: Relating students' information processing to click behaviors exhibited in the MOOC, based on video lecture perception

tional system are skipping/fast watching. In this work, we try to construct students' information processing index, based on the "Limited Capacity Information Processing Approach" (Basil, 1994; Lang et al., 1996; Lang, 2000), which asserts that people independently allocate limited amount of cognitive resources to tasks from a shared pool. Figure 1 depicts this idea.

We must acknowledge the fact that video watching in MOOCs requires students to recall facts that they already know (specific chunks of declarative knowledge (Anderson, 2014). This helps them to build a mental representation of the information presented in a MOOC video lecture segment, follow and understand the concept being currently taught. However, it must be noted that depending on the a)expertise level, which decides how available the past knowledge is and how hard is it to retrieve the previously known facts, b)perception of video lecture as difficult or simple to understand, c)motivation to learn or just have a look at the video lecture to seek specific outcomes, cognitive resource allocation would vary among these time sensitive subprocesses in stage 1 and 2 of the pipeline (depicted in Figure 1). This in turn, would be reflected by the underlying non linear navigational patterns that students have, specifically the nature of clicks which they make to adjust the speed of information processing (by pausing, seeking forward/backward, ratechange clicks), as responses to the stimuli.

Consider an example of students who watch the MOOC lecture, primarily because of reasons such as gaining familiarity with the topic. Such students would purposely not allocate their processing resources to "memory" part of the information processing pipeline (encode, store, retrieve). Additionally, they will decode and process minimal information that is required to follow the story. On the contrary, students who watch the MOOC lecture, with the aim of scoring well in post-tests (MOOC quizzes and assignments), would allocate high cognitive processing to understand, learn and retain information from the lecture. Thus, such students would process information more fully and thoroughly, despite a possibility of cognitive overload.

In order to relate our behavioral actions constructed from the raw clickstream with this rich and informative stream of literature, we create a taxonomy of behavioral actions exhibited in the clickstream to construct a quantitative "Information Processing Index (IPI)". Figure 2 reflects the proposed hierarchy of information processing from high to low using linear weight assignments. We omit the line of reasoning that goes behind defining the precise position of each behavioral action in this hierarchy due to lack of space. However, the details can be found in (Sinha, 2014c). Negative weights are necessary to distinguish between "high" and "low" weights for each behavioral action. For example, if skipping=high is weighted -3, skipping=low will be weighted +3 on the information processing index. Students' infor-

mation processing index is defined as follows:
Information Processing Index (IPI) =
$(-1)^j \sum_{i=1}^{7}$ WeightAssign(Behavioral Action i),
j=1,2 depending on whether the behavioral action is weighted low or high.

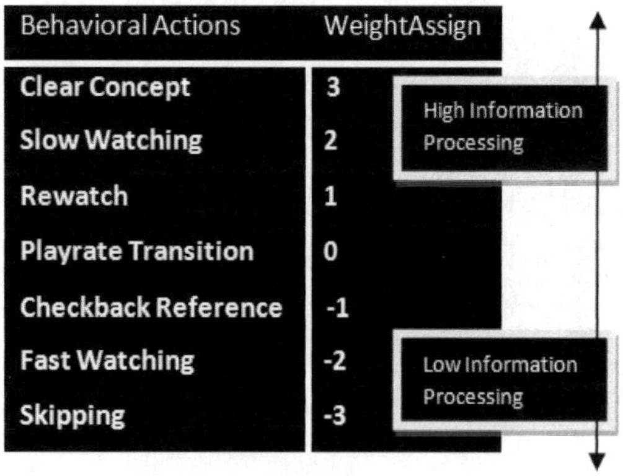

Figure 2: Linear weight assignments for behavioral clickstream actions, according to the information processing hierarchy developed

One of the focal utilities of developing such a quantitative index is that meaningful intervention could be provided in real time to students, as they steadily build up their video watching profile while interacting with MOOC video lectures. Viewing throught the lens of the Goldilocks principle (Kidd et al., 2012), our metric can potentially help instructors in understanding and differentiating between students looking away from the MOOC visual sequence, because of too simple or too complex representation. Adaptive presentation of instructional materials is another learning science application where leveraging our metric would be beneficial.

Specifically, when IPI > 0, it can be inferred that high information processing is being done by students. Therefore MOOC instructors need to check for coherency in pace of instruction delivery and students' understanding. This might also hint towards redesigning specific video lecture segments and simplifying them so that they become easier to follow. On the contrary, when IPI < 0, low information processing is being done by students. Therefore MOOC instructors need to help students better engage with the course, by providing them additional interesting reading/assignment material, or fixing video lecture content such that it captures students' attention. The neutral case of IPI = 0 occurs when students' locally exhibited high and low information processing needs in their evolving clickstream sequence counterbalance each other. So, interventions need to made depending on the video lecture segment, where IPI was >0 or <0.

4 Validation Experiments

We use machine learning to validate the methodology developed in section 3.1 and 3.2 for summarizing students' clickstream, ensuring that the same student does not appear in the train and test folds. The motivation behind setting up these experiments is to automatically measure students' length of interaction with MOOC video lectures, understand how they develop their video watching profile and discern what viewing profile of students leads to in-video and course dropouts. Furthermore, we validate the methodology developed in section 3.3 by statistically analyzing variations of IPI and testing its sensitivity to student attrition using survival models.

4.1 Machine Learning Experiment Design

4.1.1 How much do you engage?

Students, while watching MOOC video lectures can pause, seek, scroll and change rate of the video. Thus, it is meaningful to quantify students' engagement as the summation of video playing time, seeks & pauses, multiplied by the playback rate. For example, if a student plays 700 secs out of a 1000 sec video, pauses 2 times for 100 secs each, at an average play rate of 1.5, he effectively engages with the video for $(700+200)*1.5=1350$ secs. Such an interaction measure multiplied by playback rate, is representative of effective video lecture content covered.

Research Question 1: Can students' clickstream sequence predict length of students' interaction with the video lecture?

Settings: The data for this experiment comes from a randomly chosen video lecture 4-6 (6th lecture in the 4th week of the course, with not too many initial lurkers and not too many dropouts). For experimental purposes, engagement times for students are discretized by equal frequency into 2 categories (High/Low). The dependent variable is student engagement (High: 1742 examples, Low: 1741 examples). L2 regularized Logistic Regression is used as the training algorithm (with 10 fold cross validation annotated by student-id and rare feature extraction threshold being 2). As features, we extract N-grams of length 4 and 5, sequence length and regular expressions from students' clickstream sequences. In the changed setup, we consider summarized behavioral action vectors (output from level 2) as column features.

4.1.2 Are you bored or challenged?

Next, we focus our attention on how clickstream sequences evolve. If we know that students' interaction with the video lecture is going to be for a long time (reflected by high engagement), it could have been the case that they were struggling at the current level of instruction (for example, a high combination of pause/seek backward events). Therefore, if such a phenomenon can be detected in real time video lecture interaction, such learners can be presented with reinforcement course material before moving forward. Alternatively, if we know that students' interaction with the video lecture is going to be for a short time (reflected by low engagement), they could be bored or are quite likely to skip course content forward often. Such students can be presented with advanced study material. However, in order to develop such a real time knowledge model and tailor targeted interventions at students, we need to study the trajectory of click sequence formation.

Research Question 2: Can we precisely predict what will be the next sequence of clicks that leads students to different engagement states?

Settings: The data for this experiment comes from the same video lecture 4-6 (6th lecture in the 4th week of the course). The dependent variable is next click state of students (Pa, Pl, Sf, SSf, Sb, SSb, Rf, Rs). L2 regularized Logistic Regression is used as the training algorithm (with 5 fold cross validation annotated by student-id and rare feature extraction threshold being 5). If we want to predict the click at the ith instant, we extract the following features from 0 till $(i-1)^{th}$ instant: a)Engagement with the video lecture as defined for Research Question 1(High/Low); b)Proportion of click events belonging to Pl/Pa/Sf/SSf/Sb/SSb/Rf/Rs (representative of kind of interaction with the stimulus); c)N-grams of length 4,5 and sequence length from students' clickstream sequences. In the changed setup, we consider summarized behavioral action vectors (output from level 2) as column features.

4.1.3 Will you drop out of the video?

As students progress through the video, they slowly build up their video watching profile by interacting with the stimulus in different proportions, which in turn depend on their click action sequences. This motivates our next machine learning experiment, which seeks to derive utility from the first two experiments. Navigating away from the video without completing it fully is an outcome of low student engagement. A student is more likely to watch till the end of a video, if the lecture activates his thinking. Thus, it would be interesting to investigate, whether the nature of students' interaction provides us a hint about in-video dropout behavior. Prior work has made a preliminary study on how in-video dropout is correlated with length of the video, and how in-video dropout varies among first time watchers and rewatchers (Kim et al., 2014a). However, we consider video interaction features at a much finer granularity, representative of how students progress through the video. In doing so, we use detailed clickstream information, including seek, scroll and ratechange behavior, in addition to merely play and pause information.

Research Question 3: What video watching profile of students leads to in-video dropouts?

Settings: The data for this experiment comes from the same video lecture 4-6 (6th lecture in the 4th week of the course). The dependent variable is the binary variable, in-video dropout (0/1). To address the skewed class distribution, cost sensitive L2 regularized Logistic Regression is used as the training algorithm (with 10 fold cross validation annotated by student-id and rare feature extraction threshold being 2). To extract the interaction footprint of students before they drop out of the video, we extract the following features: a)N-grams of length 4,5 and sequence length from students' clickstream sequences; b)Proportion of click events belonging to Pl/Pa/Sf/SSf/Sb/SSb/Rf/Rs (representative of kind of interaction with the stimulus); c)Engagement with the video lecture as defined for Research Question 1(High/Low); e)Last click action before dropout happened; f)Time spent after the last click action was made (discretized by equal frequency to High/Low). In the changed setup, we consider summarized behavioral action vectors (output from level 2) as column features.

4.1.4 Will you watch videos and stay till the course end?

We may expect that when students find the course too tough to follow, uninteresting or boring, they will not engage with future videos. On the contrary, when students seem very interested in understanding the video and exhibit lots of rewatching behavior, we might expect them to stay on till the course end video lectures. Students who do not stay till the last week of the course (exhibit any video lecture viewing), are considered as complete course dropouts. One principal application of detecting these dropouts early could be recommendation of selected future video lectures to watch (for example, where an interesting concept, case study or application is going to be discussed), to positively motivate and pull these students back into the MOOC.

Research Question 4: Can we discover patterns in the video watching trajectory of students that can predict when are students most likely not to view future video lectures?

Settings: The data for this experiment comes from all 48 videos of "Functional Programming in Scala" MOOC (4710 non-dropouts, 9596 dropouts). To address the skewed class distribution, cost sensitive L2 regularized Logistic Regression is used as the training algorithm (with 5 fold cross validation annotated by student-id and rare feature extraction threshold being 5). The dependent variable is the binary variable, complete course dropout (0/1), indicating whether the student ultimately stayed on (watched any video lecture) till the last course week. Engagement (time in seconds) of a student is discretized by equal frequency into High and Low categories, considering all interactions in each video lecture separately (because length of each video differs, so the discretization criteria would also differ for each video). Video play proportion((video played length/video length)*100*average play rate) for a student is discretized by equal width (Very Low: <50%, Low: 50-100%, High: 100-150%, Very High: >150%). IPI for a student is discretized by equal frequency (Very Low: <-1.00, Low: [-1.00, 1.00], High: [1.00, 3.00], Very High: >3.00). The discretization criteria (equal width, frequency and number of bins) was experimentally determined. Development of trajectories for each of these factors is indicated in Figure 3. To extract the interaction footprint of students before they drop out of the course, we extract the following features: a)N-grams of length 4,5 and sequence length from "Engagement trajectory", "Video Play Proportion trajectory" and "IPI trajectory" of students for the videos watched from 0 to (n-1)th instant, b)Engagement, Video Play Proportion and IPI trajectories for the nth instance (attribute for the last video lecture watched before dropping out), c)Proportion of different symbol representations in the trajectories (for example, in a trajectory such as HLLHH, proportion(H)=60%, proportion(L)=40%.

Videos Watched	Video 1	Video 5	Video 6	Video 9...
Engagement	High	Low	Low	High..
Engagement Trajectory	H L L H...			
Video Play Prop (Vpp)	High	Very Low	Low	Very High..
Engagement Trajectory	H VL L VH...			
IPI	Very High	Low	Very Low	High..
IPI Trajectory	VH L VL H...			

Figure 3: Example depicting how different operationalized trajectories of students are formed

4.2 Results

Results of the four machine learning experiments, along with the most representative (weighted) features that characterize classes, are reported in table 2. There are two important positives here: a)The summarized behavioral action vectors from level 2 are able to achieve nearly similar values of accuracy and kappa when compared to the raw level clicks. This means that we can reason different meaningful video viewing behaviors of students without getting our hands dirty in examining noisy and continually occurring raw clicks, b)Our metric of interest, i.e the false negative rate[1] is lower for Case 1.B and Case 3.B, as compared to Case 1.A and Case 3.A, which shows the effectiveness of the clickstream summarization approach (level 2) in pre-deciphering the fate of students to some extent.

Additionally, we leverage a statistical analysis technique referred as survival analysis (Miller, 2011), to quantify the extent to which our summarized behavioral clickstream action vectors and IPI are sensitive to students' dropout. In this modeling scheme, dropout variable is 1 on the students' last week of active participation (in terms of video lecture viewing), and is 0 for all other weeks. Our investigation results indicate that a)Students'

[1]False negative rate of 0.x means that we correctly identify (100-(100*0.x))% of dropouts

Research Question	Condition	Accuracy Kappa	False Negative Rate	Most representative (weighted) features that characterize classes
1. Engagement Prediction	A)Raw Clicks	0.81 0.63	**0.24**	**High** (skipping=low, playrate transition=low, rewatch=high, slow watching=low, checkback reference=low, clear concept=high)
	B)Summarized Behavioral Action Vectors	0.75 0.49	**0.15**	**Low** (skipping=high, playrate transition=high, rewatch=low, slow watching=high, checkback reference=high, clear concept=low)
2. Next Click Prediction	A)Raw Clicks	0.68 0.57	-	**SeekFw** (playratetransition=low, skipping=low, fast watching=high, clearconcept=low) **SeekBw** (checkbackreference=high, rewatch=low, playratetransition=low, propSeekBw, clearconcept=high)
	B)Summarized Behavioral Action Vectors	0.66 0.54	-	**Ratechangefast** (playratetransition=high, rewatch=low, checkbackreference=low) **Ratechangeslow** (playratetransition=high, clearconcept=high)
3. In-video dropout Prediction	A)Raw Clicks	0.90 0.69	**0.19**	**Non dropouts** (skipping=low, clearconcept=high, slow watching=high, Checkbackreference=low, rewatch=high, engagementfromStart=low, engagementlastClick=high)
	B)Summarized Behavioral Action Vectors	0.90 0.70	**0.15**	**Dropouts** (skipping=high, clearconcept=low, slow watching=low, engagementfromStart=high, rewatch=low, engagementlastClick=low, checkbackreference=high)
4. Complete Course dropout Prediction	Operationalized trajectories	0.80 0.57	**0.143**	**Non dropouts** (trajectory_IPI=H H H H, trajectory_eng=H H H VL H, trajectory_vpp=H H H L H) **Dropouts** (trajectory_IPI=H H VL VL VL, trajectory_eng=H L H L L, trajectory_vpp=H H H H VL)

Table 2: Performance metrics for machine learning experiments. Random baseline performance is 0.5

dropout in the MOOC is 37% less likely, if they have one standard deviation greater IPI than average (Hazard ratio: 0.6367, $p<0.001$). Such students grapple more with the course material to achieve their desired learning outcomes (as reflected by their video lecture participation), b)If students' rewatching behavior changes from low to high, they are 33% less likely to dropout (Hazard ratio: 0.6734, $p<0.001$), c)As students start watching more proportion of the video lecture, they are 37% less likely to dropout of the MOOC (Hazard ratio: 0.6334, $p<0.001$). This is indicative of their continued interest in the video lecture.

Next, to discern how IPI fluctuates among different student partitions and validate whether our operationalization produces meaningful results, we plot figures 4, 5 and perform statistical tests, specifically z test (testing significance of difference between means for large sample sizes, when population standard deviation is known). Population refers to all students in the MOOC being currently studied. The right half of figure 4 depicts the variation of average IPI, among high versus low engagers and in-video dropouts versus non dropouts, in the same video lecture 4-6 from the course, that we have been performing our experiments on. Similar findings were also confirmed with other randomly chosen course videos. The left half of figure 4 shows the frequency distribution of average IPI. This figure concurs with our intuitions. The average IPI is significantly higher for students with "High" engagement ($|z|$=8.296, $p<0.01$) and "Non In-video dropouts" ($|z|$=22.54, $p<0.01$). This is also reflected in the histogram, which clearly shows that many non in-video dropouts have positive IPI that pushes up the average. Because the effect is smaller in low engagers versus high engagers, we see a more similar frequency distribution of average information processing indices in these 2 bins, as compared to contrasting differences in the histogram for in-video dropouts and non dropouts. In order to generalize these findings, we also look at the variations of average IPI among some other student partitions that we made for the whole course. "Viewers" are students who have watched or interacted with some video lecture but have not done the exercises; the "Active" students additionally turn in homework also. MOOC dropouts are those students who cease to actively participate in the MOOC (we are concerned with video lecture viewing only) before

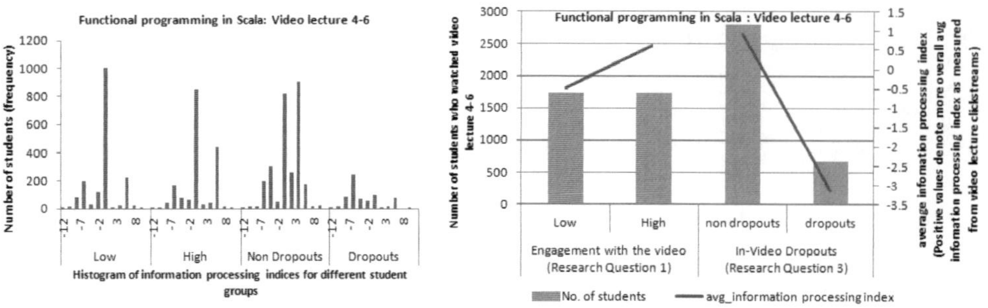

Figure 4: Variation of Average Information Processing Indices(IPI) for Video 4-6

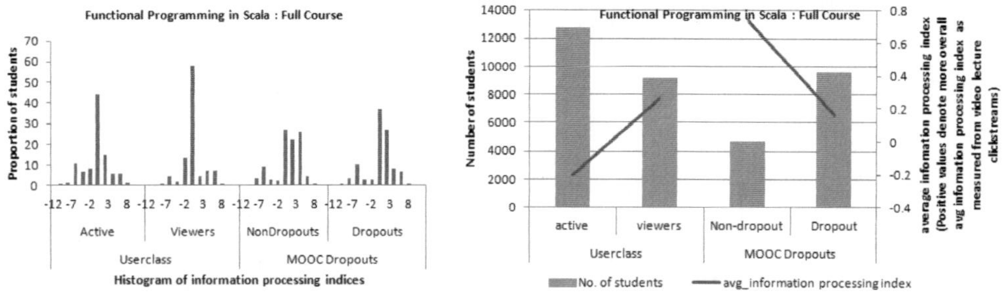

Figure 5: Variation of Average Information Processing Indices(IPI) for the full course

the last week, i.e, students who do not finish the course. An important observation in figure 5 is that IPI is clearly able to distinguish between Non-dropouts and Dropouts ($|z|$=9.06, $p<0.01$). This is also reflected in the histogram in the left half of figure 5, which verifies that more "Non dropouts" have positive IPI. More is the information processing done by students, greater is the video lecture involvement, higher are the chances to derive true utility from video lecture and remain excited and motivated to stay in the course. We also obtain striking differences between "Active" versus "Viewers" ($|z|$=10.45, $p<0.01$). Intuitively too, we expect "Viewers" to have higher IPI than "Active" class, because as their primary MOOC activity, "Viewers" grapple more with the video lecture.

5 Conclusion

In this work, we have begun to lay a foundation for research investigating students' information processing behavior while interacting with MOOC video lectures. Focusing the center of gravity on the human mind, we applied a cognitive video watching model to explain the dynamic process of cognition involved in MOOC video clickstream interaction. This paved way for the development of a simple, yet potent IPI using linear weight assignments, which can be effectively used as an operationalization for making predictions regarding critical learner behavior. We could contemplate that IPI significantly varies among different student partitions. This actually happens because of presence of smaller substructures inside these larger groupings, that are similar in their click behaviors. Deciphering unique ways of video lecture interaction in such smaller clusters using approaches such as Markov based clustering, would be very meaningful for course instructors, to design customized learning solutions for students within them (Sinha, 2014c). It would make sense to incorporate student demographics to better understand some latent factors, such as playback speed choices due to native language differences versus engagement etc. In our recent work (Sinha et al., 2014), we have been seeking to gain better visibility into how combined representations of video clickstream behavior and discussion forum footprint can provide insights on interaction pathways that lead students to central activities.

References

Anderson, A., Huttenlocher, D., Kleinberg, J., & Leskovec, J. (2014, April). "Engaging with massive online courses". *In Proceedings of the 23rd international conference on World wide web* (pp. 687-698). International World Wide Web Conferences Steering Committee.

Anderson, J. R. (2014). "Rules of the mind". *Psychology Press.*

Banerjee, A., & Ghosh, J. (2000). "Concept-based clustering of clickstream data".

Basil, M. D. (1994). "Multiple resource theory I application to television viewing". *Communication Research*, 21(2), 177-207

Belanger, Y., & Thornton, J. (2013). "Bioelectricity: A Quantitative Approach Duke Universitys First MOOC".

Brinton, C. G., Chiang, M., Jain, S., Lam, H., Liu, Z., & Wong, F. M. F. (2013). "Learning about social learning in moocs: From statistical analysis to generative model". *arXiv preprint arXiv:1312.2159.*

Cacioppo, J. T., and Wendi L. G. (1999). "Emotion". *Annual Reviews: Psychology*, 50, 191-214.

Carini, R. M., Kuh, G. D., & Klein, S. P. (2006). "Student engagement and student learning: Testing the linkages". *Research in Higher Education*, 47(1), 1-32.

Chi, M. T. (2000). "Self-explaining expository texts: The dual processes of generating inferences and repairing mental models". *Advances in instructional psychology*, 5, 161-238.

Clow, D. (2013). "MOOCs and the funnel of participation" *In Proceedings of the Third International Conference on Learning Analytics and Knowledge*, pp. 185-189. ACM

Coetzee, D., Fox, A., Hearst, M. A., & Hartmann, B. (2014, February). "Should your MOOC forum use a reputation system?". *In Proceedings of the 17th ACM conference on Computer supported cooperative work & social computing* (pp. 1176-1187). ACM.

Davis, H. C., Dickens, K., Leon Urrutia, M., Vera, S., del Mar, M., & White, S. (2014). "MOOCs for Universities and Learners An analysis of motivating factors".

Fischer, G. (2011). "Understanding, fostering, and supporting cultures of participation". *Interactions* 18, no. 3: 42-53.

Guo, P. J., & Reinecke, K. (2014, March). "Demographic differences in how students navigate through MOOCs". *In Proceedings of the first ACM conference on Learning@ scale conference* (pp. 21-30). ACM.

Guo, Philip J., Juho Kim, and Rob Rubin. (2014). "How video production affects student engagement: An empirical study of mooc videos" *ACM Learing at Scale(L@S)*, pp. 41-50.

Haggard, S., S. Brown, R. Mills, A. Tait, S. Warburton, W. Lawton, and T. Angulo. (2013). "The maturing of the MOOC: Literature review of Massive Open Online Courses and other forms of online distance learning" *BIS Research Paper 130*

Huang, J., Dasgupta, A., Ghosh, A., Manning, J., & Sanders, M. (2014, March). "Superposter behavior in MOOC forums". *In Proceedings of the first ACM conference on Learning@ scale conference* (pp. 117-126). ACM.

Kidd, C., Piantadosi, S. T., & Aslin, R. N. (2012). "The Goldilocks effect: Human infants allocate attention to visual sequences that are neither too simple nor too complex". *PLoS One*, 7(5), e36399.

Kim, J., Guo, P. J., Seaton, D. T., Mitros, P., Gajos, K. Z., & Miller, R. C. (2014a, March). "Understanding in-video dropouts and interaction peaks inonline lecture videos". *In Proceedings of the first ACM conference on Learning@ scale conference* (pp. 31-40). ACM.

Kim, J., Shang-Wen L., Carrie J. C., Krzysztof Z. G., Robert C. M. (2014b). "Leveraging Video Interaction Data and Content Analysis to Improve Video Learning" *CHI 2014 Workshop on Learning Innovation at Scale*

Kulkarni, C. E., Socher, R., Bernstein, M. S., & Klemmer, S. R. (2014, March). "Scaling short-answer grading by combining peer assessment with algorithmic scoring". *In Proceedings of the first ACM conference on Learning@ scale conference* (pp. 99-108). ACM.

Lang, A., John N., and Byron R. (1996). "Negative video as structure: Emotion, attention, capacity, and memory". *Journal of Broadcasting & Electronic Media*, 40(4), 460-477

Lang, A. (2000). "The limited capacity model of mediated message processing". *Journal of communication*, 50(1), 46-70.

Lie M. T., Debjanee B., Judy K. (2014). "Online learning at scale: user modeling requirements towards motivation and personalisation". *In Learning Innovations at Scale CHI' 14 Workshop*

Miller Jr, Rupert G. (2011). "Survival analysis". Vol. 66. *John Wiley & Sons*

Nawrot, I., and Antoine D. (2014). "Building engagement for MOOC students: introducing support for time management on online learning platforms." *In Proceedings of the companion publication of the 23rd international conference on World wide web companion*, pp. 1077-1082.

North, S. M., Ronny R., and Max M. N. (2014). "To Adapt MOOCS, or Not? That is No Longer the Question." *Universal Journal of Educational Research* 2(1): 69-72

Ramesh, A., Goldwasser, D., Huang, B., Daum H. III, and Getoor, L. (2013). "Modeling Learner Engagement in MOOCs using Probabilistic Soft Logic". *In NIPS Workshop on Data Driven Education*

Schmidt, D. C., and Zach M. (2013). "Producing and Delivering a Coursera MOOC on Pattern-Oriented Software Architecture for Concurrent and Networked Software"

Sinha, T., Banka, A., Kang, D. K., (2013). "Leveraging user profile attributes for improving pedagogical accuracy of learning pathways". *In Proceedings of 3rd Annual International Conference on Education and E-Learning(EeL 2013)*, Singapore

Sinha, T. (2014a). "Together we stand, Together we fall, Together we win: Dynamic team formation in massive open online courses" *In Fifth International Conference on the Applications of Digital Information and Web Technologies (ICADIWT)* pp. 107-112. IEEE

Sinha, T. (2014b). "Supporting MOOC Instruction with Social Network Analysis". *arXiv preprint arXiv:1401.5175*

Sinha, T. (2014c). "Your click decides your fate": Leveraging clickstream patterns from MOOC videos to infer students' information processing & attrition behavior. *arXiv preprint arXiv:1407.7143.*

Sinha, T., Li, N., Jermann, P., Dillenbourg, P. (2014). Capturing attrition intensifying structural traits from didactic interaction sequences of MOOC learners. *Proceedings of the 2014 Empirical Methods in Natural Language Processing Workshop on Modeling Large Scale Social Interaction in Massively Open Online Courses*, Qatar, October 2014

Tillmann, N., De Halleux, J., Xie, T., Gulwani, S., and Bishop, J. (2013). "Teaching and learning programming and software engineering via interactive gaming". *In ICSE*, 11171126

Van der L., Mark PJ. (2014). "The stringdist Package for Approximate String Matching" *The R Journal*

Wang, G., Tristan K., Christo W., Xiao W., Haitao Z., and Ben Y. Z. (2013). "You are how you click: Clickstream analysis for sybil detection" *In USENIX Security Symposium* (Washington, DC)

Yang, D., Sinha T., Adamson D., and Rose C. P. (2013). "Turn on, Tune in, Drop out: Anticipating student dropouts in Massive Open Online Courses" *In NIPS Workshop on Data Driven Education*

Identifying Student Leaders from MOOC Discussion Forums through Language Influence

Seungwhan Moon **Saloni Potdar** **Lara Martin**
Language Technology Institute
Carnegie Mellon University
5000 Forbes Avenue, Pittsburgh, PA, 15213
{seungwhm, spotdar, ljmartin}@cs.cmu.edu

Abstract

Identifying and understanding the motivations of *student leaders* from Massively Open Online Course (MOOC) discussion forums provides the key to making the online learning environment engaging, collaborative, and instructive. In this paper, we propose to identify student leaders solely based on textual features, or specifically by analyzing how they *influence* other students' language. We propose an improved method of measuring language accommodation based on people's choice of words given a semantic topic of interest, and show that student leaders indeed coordinate other students' language usage. We also show that our proposed method can successfully distinguish student leaders from the two MOOC discussion forum datasets.

1 Introduction

One of the challenges Massively Open Online Courses (MOOCs) face is that they lack a physical medium that enables active real-time interaction between students and instructors, especially when compared to the offline learning environment. While online discussion forums in MOOCs play an important role in bridging this gap, the "massiveness" of the student size makes it hard for instructors to provide sufficient feedback or answers to students' questions in a timely manner.

It is often the *student leaders* who accommodate this situation by voluntarily helping other students and answering their questions in discussion forums. The student leaders encourage other students to participate in the discussion and make the online learning experience much more collaborative and engaging. Therefore, it is important to identify student leaders and understand their motivations, thus promoting more students to act like leaders. Identifying leadership in MOOCs also brings new insights to the multi-dimensional evaluation of students in online courses. This significantly builds upon previous literature that evaluates students taking MOOCs solely based on their task-oriented performance (Foltz and Rosenstein, 2013; Basu et al., 2013).

Identifying student leaders in MOOC courses is a challenging task, as illustrated in Figure 1. While most of the student leaders actively interact with other students in a large cluster of people, some student leaders only lead a small clique of students. Activeness of student participation cannot be a sole measure to identify student leaders, because there are a number of active 'questioners' who exhibit very different motivations from student leaders. This challenge inspires us to look closely at the *language* of the leaders in order to identify them.

The task of identifying leaders has been well studied in various domains, but the challenge is often unique to the specific property of an online network or a community. For example, a frequency-based data mining approach has been proven particularly successful for a social network with a strong visibility control (e.g. a friend network) and a discrete set of user actions (e.g. sharing of a post, etc.) (Goyal et al., 2008; Bodendorf and Kaiser, 2009; Shafiq et al., 2013). In their work, they identify leaders by tracking how a certain action gets shared and propagated among a given network of users. However, it is challenging to apply this approach for identifying leaders from MOOC discussion forums, because a visibility network of users or community actions are not clearly defined in MOOCs.

For an online community forum where the query information and use pattern are accessible, several studies have proposed to use the link structure and the topic information about users to identify opinion leaders (Li et al., 2013; Pal and Kon-

Proceedings of the 2014 Conference on Empirical Methods in Natural Language Processing (EMNLP), pages 15–20,
October 25-29, 2014, Doha, Qatar.

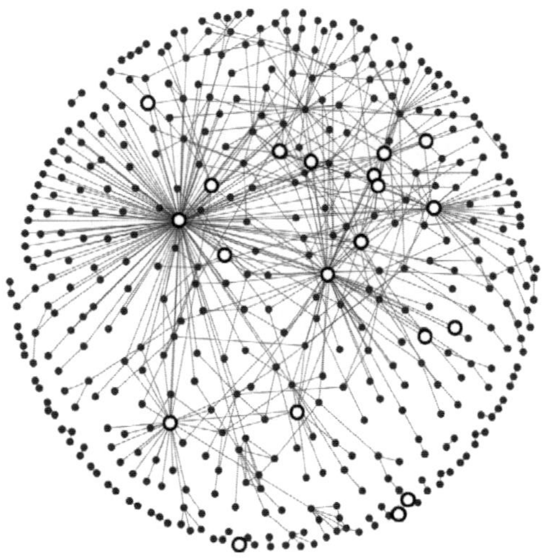

Figure 1: An interaction graph of the Python MOOC discussion forum where each node and edge represents a student and an interaction of two students within the forum (e.g. enough number of conversation exchanges above a threshold), respectively. Larger white nodes refer to the annotated student leaders. While most of the leaders are highly connected (actively interacting with other students), note that the white nodes may also appear in small cliques as well. Some of the highly connected nodes are not labeled as leaders, whom we refer to as active 'questioners'.

stan, 2010; Sharara et al., 2011). They employ features such as PageRank, HITS, and other non-linguistic features such as longevity (how long the person has stayed on the forum), etc., all of which serve as a cue in determining and identifying the extent of users' expertise and influence.

While some of the MOOC datasets provide this information, in this paper we only focus on the textual features of the MOOC discussion forums so that we can target general MOOC datasets. We show that we can identify leaders as role models who influence through language, and show how a community norm may form within a short life span of an online course via student leaders. We also propose a new approach to measure language accommodation which in our experiment furthers the previous literature on the subject.

The rest of the paper is organized as follows: Section 2 explains in detail the approach that we propose to identify leaders. Section 3 gives a brief overview of the two MOOC datasets from different courses, and we present our empirical evaluation in Section 4 on these datasets. Finally, we give our concluding remarks and proposed future work in Section 5.

2 Methods

It is well studied by the linguistics community that people tend to mimic the style of speech or choices of words made by the people that they are communicating with (Niederhoffer and Pennebaker, 2002). This phenomena is called *language coordination*, which is frequently observed especially when there are power differences within the conversation participants (Danescu-Niculescu-Mizil and Lee, 2011; Danescu-Niculescu-Mizil et al., 2012). We hypothesize that the power difference may arise within the students as well, especially through *dependence*: if a student A needs knowledge from a student B, and is thus dependent on B, this gives B a temporary power over A. As such, we identify a set of student leaders by how much other students accommodate their language when they converse with student leaders.

In order to measure students' language coordination towards student leaders, we take the similar approach proposed by (Danescu-Niculescu-Mizil et al., 2012). In their work, they provide a concise probabilistic coordination measure which defines language coordination from a speaker to a target on a set of function words. Specifically, they use 8 pre-defined categories and a total of 451 lexemes as a set of function words to track the language influence. Their proposed accommodation measure is shown to be successful in distinguishing the individuals of different power status. While this work bases its motivation from a specific line of work in the linguistics that defines particular function words as markers for influence, it does not fully capture the broad range of linguistic behaviors that are reported as language accommodation (Baxter and Braithwaite, 2008; Hall, 2008).

In this paper, we propose to measure language coordination based on people's choice of words, given a specific *theme*. Consider word clusters learned from a large corpus, where words are grouped by their semantic similarity. During a conversation between a speaker A and a target B, they can draw words from any cluster, which is analogous to choosing a topic or theme to discuss. Given a theme, people may choose any words from the chosen cluster, all of which have a semantically similar meaning. However, if A follows B's specific choice of words given a cluster, we consider this action as evidence for language accommodation of A towards B. Based on the probabilistic analysis, we measure the overall language coordination for each conversation participant. Note that this definition of language accommodation can capture language coordination beyond the use of particular function words, and provide a way to analyze broader language influence that is unique to the community. Figure 2 shows the illustration of this approach.

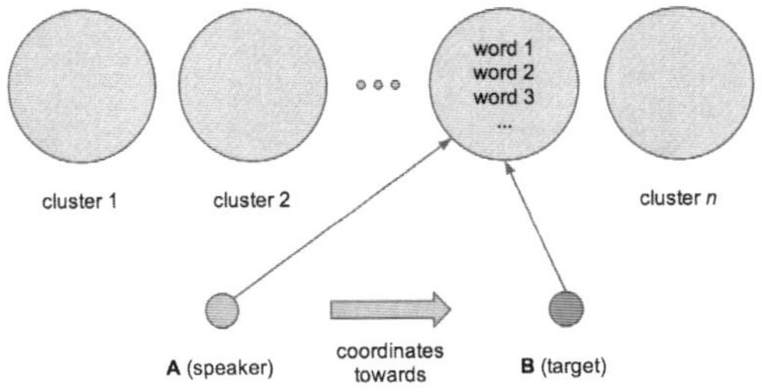

Figure 2: Language accommodation based on people's choice of words given a theme (cluster). Words are clustered based on their semantic similarity. If A (speaker) follows B (target)'s specific choice of word from a cluster, given all the other options of similar words within the same cluster, we define this action as language accommodation of A towards B.

To cluster words based on their syntactic and semantic similarity, we take the approach by (Mikolov et al., 2013a; Mikolov et al., 2013b) which maps words into high-dimensional vectors based on their statistical occurrence in relation to other words in a sentence. We then use the K-means clustering algorithm (MacQueen, 1967) to group the words by their Euclidean distance within the semantic space. To reduce the computational complexity, we pick the 20 most frequent clusters from the dataset that we analyze, and we use the words in those clusters as markers to track language coordination.

We then borrow the definition of language accommodation measure by (Danescu-Niculescu-Mizil et al., 2012), and define the language coordination of a speaker a towards a target b on a marker w_k (that belongs to a word cluster k) as follows:

$$C^{w_k}(a \to b) = P(E^{w_k}_{u_a \to u_b} | E^{w_k}_{u_b}) - P(E^{w_k}_{u_a \to u_b})$$

where a is the speaker that coordinates towards the target b, $E^{w_k}_{u_a \to u_b}$ is the event that the utterance of a exhibits a linguistic marker w_k in its reply to the utterance of b, and $E^{w_k}_{u_b}$ is the event that the utterance of b exhibits a marker w_k. The conversation set is defined over the exchanges that contain the words from a given cluster k.

In a thread-based discussion forum like the MOOC datasets, however, it is ambiguous to tell who is talking with whom. Therefore, we define the conversational exchange between b and a if b's post appears after a's post in the same thread.

3 MOOC Dataset

In this section, we describe the two MOOC online discussion forum datasets we used in our studies. The datasets consist of the conversations from two courses from Coursera[1]: *Learn to Program: The Fundamentals* (Python) and *Introduction to Psychology as a Science* (Psychology). The Python course consists of 3,509 students, 7 instructors and 24,963 posts across 10 weeks. Each thread consists of replies and comments along with a username associated with it. The Psychology course spans over 12 weeks and has 1,982 students and 3 instructors. In our studies, we focus on the interaction between three groups of people: instructors (including professors and teaching assistants), student leaders, and non-leaders. In order to evaluate the performance of the proposed method on the MOOC discussion forums, we have hand-annotated leaders and non-leaders from a subset of the student pool.

4 Results and Discussion

We test the following two hypotheses on language accommodation: (1) students coordinate more towards student leaders than towards non-student leaders (H_{target}), and (2) student leaders coordinate towards other students less than non-student leaders coordinate towards other students ($H_{speaker}$). Figure 3 shows the language accommodation of three different groups (instructors, leaders, and non-leaders) with other students that are not labeled as any group. We provide the results for the case when we apply our *cluster-based* accommodation measure to test H_{target} and $H_{speaker}$, and for when we use the function words as markers to track accommodation (Danescu-Niculescu-Mizil et al., 2012). For the *cluster-*

[1] https://www.coursera.org, one of the leading MOOC providers

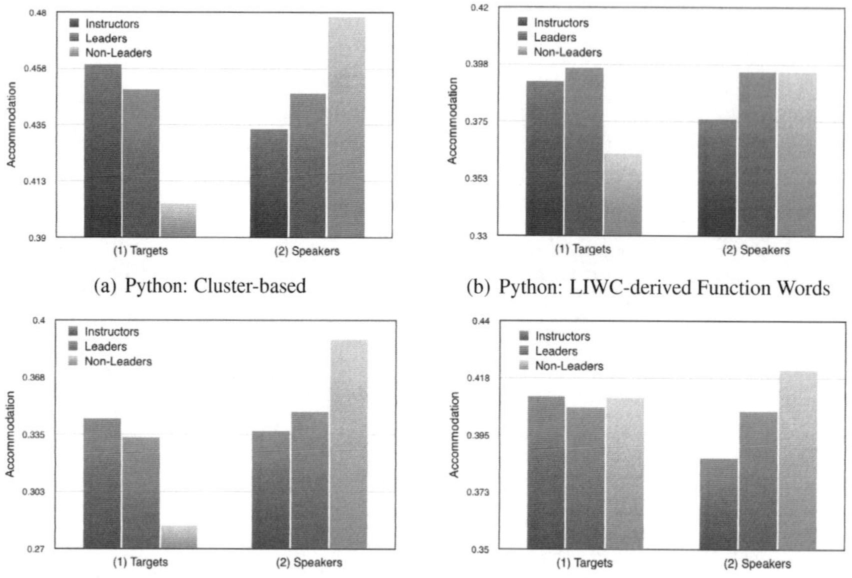

(a) Python: Cluster-based

(b) Python: LIWC-derived Function Words

(c) Psychology: Cluster-based

(d) Psychology: LIWC-derived Function Words

Figure 3: The aggregated language accommodation measurement using (a), (c): cluster-based and (b), (d): LIWC-derived lexemes, (1) from students towards each target class (testing H_{target}) and (2) from each speaker class towards students (testing $H_{speaker}$), for the Python and the Psychology datasets.

based method, we use `word2vec`[2] which provides the word vectors trained on the *Google News* corpus (about 100 billion words) (Mikolov et al., 2013b). Table 1 directly shows the difference between the two methods.

Figure 3 shows that student leaders influence other students' language more than non-leaders do ($p < 0.05$), supporting our first hypothesis H_{target}. It can also be seen that the language of non-leaders coordinates towards that of other students more than the language of student leaders does ($p < 0.05$), supporting our second hypothesis $H_{speaker}$. Note that instructors and leaders exhibit almost the same behavior in terms of language accommodation. These results coincide with the observation that student leaders and instructors play a similar role in discussion forums. In addition, while both word cluster-based and LIWC-derived methods support our hypotheses, the distinction seen is more significant in the result from our cluster-based method (summarized in Table 1). These results indicate that the proposed method of measuring accommodation can capture the language influence more accurately than the previous method.

Based on our proposed measure of language accommodation, we were able to see how language influence is accumulated throughout the lifetime of the community. Figure 4 shows that the language coordination of students towards student leaders decreases as the course progresses, eventually converging to the level of language coordination from students to non-student leaders. The same convergence behavior can be observed from the language coordination of student leaders and non-leaders towards students as well. This result indicates that the distinction between students and non-student leaders becomes less significant in terms of their language influence. This result can also be interpreted as a community norm being formed throughout the course, which was initiated by student leaders at first. While MOOC courses have a relatively short lifespan, the results make intuitive sense because they often include technical jargon (e.g. the programming related words for Python MOOC course) which can be quickly learned by community members.

Table 2 shows the prediction accuracy on the task of differentiating between a student leader and a non-leader given a set of conversation exchanges between two people (a,b) with different status. We used the following features as input to an SVM classifier. *Cluster* uses the binary fea-

[2] `https://code.google.com/p/word2vec/`

		Δ Accommodation (%)	
		Cluster	LIWC
(a)	ΔC_{target}	**4.58**	3.35
	$\Delta C_{speaker}$	**-3.04**	-0.01
(b)	ΔC_{target}	**5.01**	-0.38
	$\Delta C_{speaker}$	**-4.09**	-1.62

Table 1: The difference in language accommodation measure between leaders and non-leaders for each method (cluster-based, LIWC-derived function words) on (a) Python and (b) Psychology MOOC datasets. ΔC_{target} refers to the students' language accommodation towards leaders subtracted by their language accommodation towards non-leaders. $\Delta C_{speaker}$ refers to the leaders' language accommodation towards students subtracted by non-leaders' language accommodation towards students. Higher absolute value of ΔC indicates that the method can distinguish leaders and non-leaders better.

tures that indicates whether a coordinates towards b more than b towards a on each marker from the word cluster-based method. *LIWC* uses the binary features as well, using the LIWC-derived function words as markers for accommodation. *BOW* refers to a standard bag of words feature set.

We test the performance on both in-domain and cross-domain cases using the datasets from the two different courses. While *BOW* performs significantly better than the other two coordination features-based methods for the in-domain cases, it does not generalize well for the cross-domain cases. This is because there are unique sets of technical vocabulary that are used in each respective course, which are often strong indicators of leadership or expertise in the domain. The proposed cluster-based method performs better than *LIWC* in both in-domain and cross-domain cases, showing that the proposed method better captures the leader's language influence on other students.

5 Conclusions

The main contributions of this paper are as follows: we have proposed that identifying student leaders from MOOC discussion forums is an important task that can potentially improve the quality of the courses by promoting a collaborative and engaging learning environment. We then proposed a new method to measure language accommodation based on people's choices of words given a theme. We have shown that our proposed approach can better capture the language influence than previous literature on accommodation using the two MOOC datasets. We were also able to show that a community norm can be formed throughout the course, evidenced from the time-based analysis of language accommodation.

We plan to improve this research with respect to the way we measure language accommodation. Specifically, we would like to propose a new metric for measuring language accommodation by analyzing the propagation of influence, instead of looking at conversations locally. Suppose, for in-

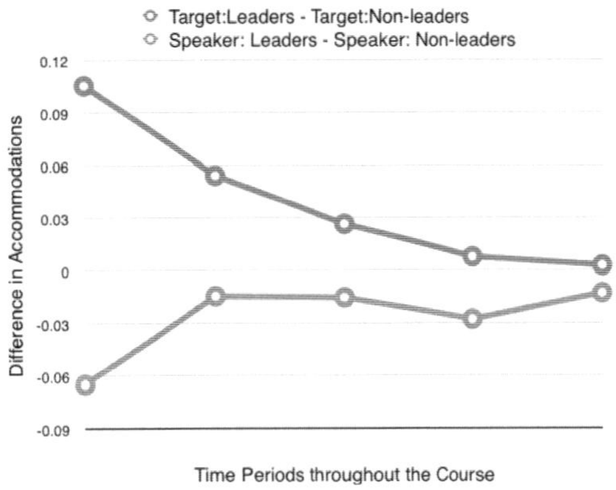

Figure 4: Language accommodation difference at each period throughout the Python course. The blue line (upper) refers to ΔC_{target}, whereas the green line (lower) refers to $\Delta C_{speaker}$. Higher absolute value of ΔC indicates that the method can distinguish leaders and non-leaders better.

	In-domain		Cross-domain	
Train:	Python	Psych	Python	Psych
Test:	Python	Psych	Psych	Python
Cluster	61.17	57.54	60.01	59.03
LIWC	58.34	55.10	58.52	57.92
BOW	73.12	69.23	53.26	54.07

Table 2: Classification accuracy of identifying a leader from a pair of students with different labeled roles. *Cluster* and *LIWC* refer to the coordination features using two different methods to track influence markers. The chance performance is 50 %.

stance, that during an online discussion a person b coordinates towards a with respect to a specific linguistic style marker m, and that within a short period of time, we find evidence that another person c coordinates towards b on the same marker m. We argue that c should be considered as pertaining to the influence graph of a, contributing to the evidence that a is a leader.

Acknowledgments

We would like to acknowledge the contributions made by Professor Carolyn Rosé for her valuable and constructive suggestions.

References

Sumit Basu, Chuck Jacobs, and Lucy Vanderwende. 2013. Powergrading: a clustering approach to amplify human effort for short answer grading. *NIPS Workshop on Data Driven Education.*

Leslie A. Baxter and Dawn O. Braithwaite. 2008. *Communication Accommodation Theory. Engaging theories in interpersonal communication: Multiple perspectives.*

Freimut Bodendorf and Carolin Kaiser. 2009. Detecting opinion leaders and trends in online social networks. In *Proceedings of the 2Nd ACM Workshop on Social Web Search and Mining*, SWSM '09, pages 65–68, New York, NY, USA. ACM.

Cristian Danescu-Niculescu-Mizil and Lillian Lee. 2011. Chameleons in imagined conversations: A new approach to understanding coordination of linguistic style in dialog. In *Proceedings of the ACL Workshop on Cognitive Modeling and Computational Linguistics*, pages 76–87.

Cristian Danescu-Niculescu-Mizil, Lillian Lee, Bo Pang, and Jon Kleinberg. 2012. Echoes of power: Language effects and power differences in social interaction. *Proceedings of WWW 2012.*

Peter W. Foltz and Mark Rosenstein. 2013. Tracking student learning in a state-wide implementation of automated writing scoring. *NIPS Workshop on Data Driven Education.*

Amit Goyal, Francesco Bonchi, and Laks V. S. Lakshmanan. 2008. Discovering leaders from community actions. *CIKM '08.*

Phil Hall. 2008. Policespeak. *Dimensions of Forensic Linguistics.*

Yanyan Li, Shaoqian Ma, Yonghe Zhang, Ronghuai Huang, and Kinshuk. 2013. An improved mix framework for opinion leader identification in online learning communities. *Knowledge-Based Systems*, 43(0):43 – 51.

J MacQueen. 1967. Some methods for classification and analysis of multivariate observations. *Proceedings of the Fifth Berkeley Symposium on Mathematical Statistics and Probability*, Volume 1: Statistics.

Tomas Mikolov, Kai Chen, Greg Corrado, and Jeffrey Dean. 2013a. Efficient estimation of word representations in vector space. *CoRR*, abs/1301.3781.

Tomas Mikolov, Ilya Sutskever, Kai Chen, Greg Corrado, and Jeffrey Dean. 2013b. Distributed representations of words and phrases and their compositionality. *Proceedings of the Advances in Neural Information Processing Systems (NIPS).*

K. G. Niederhoffer and J. W. Pennebaker. 2002. Linguistic style matching in social interaction. *Journal of Language and Social Psychology*, 21.

Aditya Pal and Joseph A. Konstan. 2010. Expert identification in community question answering: Exploring question selection bias. In *Proceedings of the 19th ACM International Conference on Information and Knowledge Management*, CIKM '10, pages 1505–1508, New York, NY, USA. ACM.

M. Zubair Shafiq, Muhammad U. Ilyas, Alex X. Liu, and Hayder Radha. 2013. Identifying leaders and followers in online social networks. *Selected Areas in Communications, IEEE Journal on (JSAC)*, 31.

Hossam Sharara, Lise Getoor, and Myra Norton. 2011. Active surveying: A probabilistic approach for identifying key opinion leaders. In *The 22nd International Joint Conference on Artificial Intelligence (IJCAI '11).*

Towards Identifying the Resolvability of Threads in MOOCs

Diyi Yang, Miaomiao Wen, Carolyn Rose
Language Technologies Institute, Carnegie Mellon University
5000 Forbes Ave, Pittsburgh, 15213
{diyiy,mwen,cprose}@cs.cmu.edu

Abstract

One important function of the discussion forums of Massive Open Online Courses (MOOCs) is for students to post problems they are unable to resolve and receive help from their peers and instructors. There are a large proportion of threads that are not resolved to the satisfaction of the students for various reasons. In this paper, we attack this problem by firstly constructing a conceptual model validated using a Structural Equation Modeling technique, which enables us to understand the factors that influence whether a problem thread is satisfactorily resolved. We then demonstrate the robustness of these findings using a predictive model that illustrates how accurately those factors can be used to predict whether a thread is resolved or unresolved. Experiments conducted on one MOOC show that thread resolveability connects closely to our proposed five dimensions and that the predictive ensemble model gives better performance over several baselines.

1 Introduction

Massive Open Online Courses (MOOCs), run by organizations such as Coursera, have been among the most news worthy social media environments in the past year. While usage of social media affordances such as discussion forums in such courses is small relative to usage of videos or assignments, participation in the discussion forums is an important predictor of commitment to the course (Yang et al., 2013). We hypothesize that supporting a positive experience in such forums has the potential to increase retention in such courses. In this paper, we specifically study the behavior of students in a MOOC course for learning Python programming. We present empirical work that elucidates an important problem in existing MOOC discussion forums, propose a practical solution, and offer promising results in a corpus based evaluation.

MOOCs for programming skills can be seen as important resources for the professional development of programmers and programmers in training. While MOOCs for learning programming are a recent phenomenon, they are not the first web accessible resources for development of such skills. In recent years, a plethora of question/answer sites for programming have become available that have grown into thriving communities of practice for programmers. In these online communities, programmers can get mentoring from those who are more expert than them and offer mentoring to programmers who are less expert than them. For example, StackOverflow[1] has become a forum not only for getting specific questions answered, but for negotiating the pros and cons of alternative ways of solving technical problems. The code proposed as part of alternative solutions remains as part of the community memory, which is then accessible for those who come later with similar concerns.

Where StackOverflow falls short is in providing an appropriate environment for the active involvement of very novice programmers. When such novices come to a forum like StackOverflow and present their naive questions, they are frequently met with sarcastic responses if they get a response at all.

MOOCs for learning programming skills fill a gap left open by such environments, in that they welcome the very novice and provide forums where naive questions are not shunned. Nevertheless, discussion forums that only include such novice programmers would be akin to *the blind leading the blind* were it not for the involvement of a few more expert students and the teaching staff. This does not fully solve the problem, however. Many threads are

[1] http://stackoverflow.com/

Proceedings of the 2014 Conference on Empirical Methods in Natural Language Processing (EMNLP), pages 21–31,
October 25-29, 2014, Doha, Qatar.

still left without a satisfactory resolution. Currently, it is challenging for the teaching staff and expert participants to know where in the massive amount of communication to look for opportunities where their support is most needed. This is the problem we aim to address in this paper, i.e. automatically identify whether a thread is resolved and provide potential for better allocation of instructor and student resources.

In the remainder of the paper we first survey related work. Next we describe the formulation of the problem. We then present a series of two experiments, the later one building on the successful findings and results from the former. The results conducted on one MOOC show that our proposed model of thread resolveability better captures the difference between resolved and unresolved threads and that the ensemble logistic model outperforms several baselines. We conclude the paper with a discussion of the limitations of this work and next steps.

2 Related Work

MOOCs have received more and more attention recently, with the promise of providing many of the benefits of traditional classroom learning but not limited by time, location or finances. Much prior work has focused on analysis of such platforms to motivate the design of better student learning experiences. In various ways, the issue of students needing support from instructors and students has been addressed (Lieberman, 1995).

An important component in the Coursera environment is the discussion forums, which students can use to learn new knowledge from each other and from the teaching staff when they participate. In support of the importance of the discussion forums in connection with major problems like attrition, models are proposed to predict student dropout based both on their video watching behavior and also discussion forum posting behavior, such as how many posts a student has made (Balakrishnan, 2013). Student behavior in the discussion forum is also focused by other prior works (Yang et al., 2013). Yang et al. analyze drop out along the way, demonstrating the predictive power of features extracted within time windows of student behavior within the forums. The results of their work suggest that interaction with other students is important for keeping students motivated, which is further confirmed by many works (Yang et al., 2014; Rosé et al., 2014). Besides, linguistic reflections are also crucial for students engagement (Wen et al., 2014).

Other work highlights the importance of interaction in the form of feedback during participation in MOOCs. For example, some prior work (Piech et al., 2013) has explored peer grading, especially in helping grading of open ended assignments, in courses with thousands or tens of thousands of students. Other work takes a more holistic approach to assessment of student behavior. For example, in one such example (Kizilcec et al., 2013), instead of looking at students' assignments, students were classified based on their patterns of interaction with video lectures and assessment activities. This behavior trace was processed using a simple and scalable classification method that could identify a small number of longitudinal engagement trajectories that potentially provide the impetus for tailored feedback or mentoring.

Outside of MOOC discussion forums, there has also been work investigating the conditions under which questions receive appropriate feedback in more general Question Answering (QA) sites. In particular, this work has been framed as research on thread resolveability in QA sites. It can be conceived as the human counterpart to fully automated question answering systems (Prager et al., 2000; Perera, 2012; Jeon et al., 2006; Agichtein et al., 2008). Much of this work has emphasized the importance of having effective features to model question and answer processes.

In some of this prior work, the focus has been on identifying whether a thread is answered given a question and a set of potential answers (Sung et al., 2013; Tian et al., 2013). The prior work (Anderson et al., 2012) has focused on understanding the dynamics of the surrounding community activity, like the process through which answers and voters arrive over time. Based on understanding of such factors, a prediction can be made about the long term value for the community of a question being answered. Similarly, Agichtein and colleagues (Agichtein et al., 2009) presented a general prediction model of information seeker satisfaction in community question answering, and developed content, structure and community focused features for the question answering task. A collection of other related work (Liu and Agichtein, 2008) has developed personalized models of asker satisfaction to predict whether a particular question starter will be satisfied with the answers given by others. This is solved by exploring content, structure and interaction features using standard prediction models.

Work on automated question answering systems can also be seen as relevant since questions that can be answered automatically do not need a human response, and therefore might reduce the load on available human effort. Instead of predicting whether a problem is answered, strategies for predicting are explored when a question answering system is likely to give an incorrect answer (Brill et al., 2002). To further understand how a question is answered, researchers (Yih et al., 2013) have studied the answer sentence selection problem for question answering and improves the model performance by using lexical semantic resources. That is, they construct semantic matches between question and answers. In terms of the extent to which the question is answered, Shah and colleagues (Shah and Pomerantz, 2010) evaluated answer quality by manually rating the quality of each answer. Then they extracted various features to train classifiers to select the best answer for that question. Liu et al. (Liu et al., 2011) proposed to use a mutual reinforcement based propagation algorithm to predict question quality based. The model makes its prediction based on the connection between askers and topics, and how those connections predict differences in quality.

The above question answering work is all about general discussion forums (Qu et al., 2009; Kabutoya et al., 2010), such as Yahoo! Answers[2]. In our work, in addition to taking advantage of existing QA work, we also adopt a linguistic perspective (Jansen et al., 2014) and take semantic matching into account using a latent semantic approach. To the best of our knowledge, this is the first work on thread resolvability analysis in a MOOC context.

3 Research Problem Introduction

In this section, we focus on how to identify the resolveability of threads in the MOOC forums. We firstly introduce the research context and dataset, then we formulate our resolveability problem.

3.1 Research Context and Dataset

In programming MOOCs, when students encounter problems working on the programming assignments, or when something is not clear from the readings or lectures, students have the opportunity to initiate a thread in the course forum, in order to engage other students in the class as well as the teaching staff. For example, if a student were confused about the distinction between an argument and a parameter in Python, he/she would post the question to the variables subforum, marking it unresolved at the same time. In the ideal case, another participant would reply to this question with some detailed explanation and example, which would solve that problem. When the student who initiated the thread receives the response, assuming it is adequate, that student may mark it as resolved. Others may join in as well, and individual posts may be rated through upvotes and downvotes. In contrast to existing QA sites, no *best answer* option is available. Thus, the resolved/unresolved button provides the closest equivalent groundtruth.

The data for this paper was crawled from a Python language course. Our focus was specifically to investigate the inner workings of threads related to getting answers to questions or help with programming difficulty. In order to avoid including threads in our dataset that are off-topic or otherwise irrelevant, we limited the set of forums to the subforums that focus strongly on course content, including those indicated to focus on lectures, exercises and assignments as well as the final exam. That is, we discarded posts in the study groups, social discussion, and other discussion areas that do not have unresolved buttons. In the final dataset, there were 2508 threads (1244 resolved threads) in total, and 2896 users (12 instructors and staffs) who had at least one post. Each question is associated with a label indicating whether it is resolved or not.

3.2 Problem Formulation

Work on the related problem of analysis of QA websites has grown in popularity in recent years. However, due to differences in how MOOCs work as temporary online communities, it is necessary to consider how findings from prior work in these areas may or may not generalize to this new context as we formulate our research problem. In particular, MOOCs are different from existing QA websites, such as Yahoo! Q&A, Stack Overflow. The purpose of QA sites is primarily for people to get answers. While people may learn from their interactions on such sites, those sites are not designed in particular to support learning. Thus,

[2]http://answers.yahoo.com/

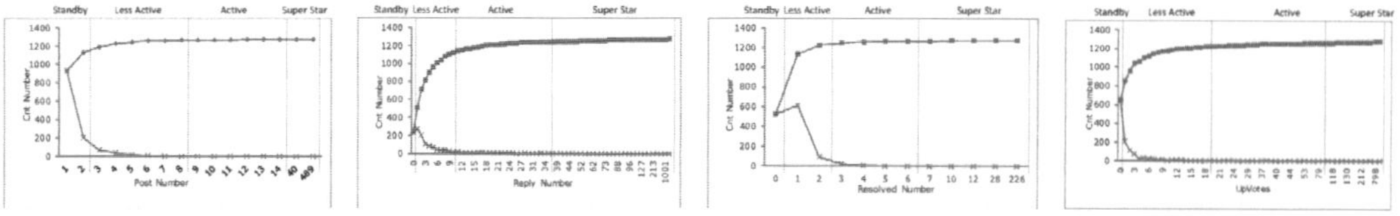

(a) Question Post (b) Reply Devotee (c) Resolved Favor (d) UpVotes

Figure 1: Starter Influence Statistics. Each Figure has two curves; the below one indicates how many users have made the associated number of posts/reply. The above one is the cumulative version of the same.

different characteristics are needed in the MOOCs discussion threads. One implication is that the discussions in MOOCs may need to be more interactive than those found in environments such as StackOverflow. Students who post problems can be expected to be less capable of fully comprehending an answer even if it is a good one. This demands more effort from those with the ability to offer helpful responses. In order for the discussions to be effective, the threads must include a balance of naive participants and participants with more knowledge. A related issue is that it is not yet ubiquitous for participants in MOOCs to have the opportunity to earn a reputation score for offering useful answers and other instructional support. In other QA sites, this is both a valuable motivator as well as an important predictor of resolved versus unresolved question threads (Anderson et al., 2012). Thus, students who post questions may need to sell their problem in order to attract those who can offer help. Taking these interrelated issues into account, an important aspect of our modeling work is in recognizing the different roles that users play in the community. Related to this, we will describe below how we develop models that include latent variables related to the propensity of users to initiate problem threads that attract useful responses, and the propensity of others to contribute useful responses in such contexts. We refer to these complementary variables as *starter influence* and *expert participation* respectively.

Secondly, all are welcome to learn in a MOOC and participate actively even if they have no prior knowledge. In an educational context, it would not be appropriate to meet a naive question with a sarcastic response. In contrast, in Stack Overflow, it would be treated as unremarkable for a naive question to get a sarcastic response. While naive participants may not enjoy such responses, they learn to expect them. Since approaching posted problems with patience and friendliness is important for avoiding discouraging new learners, we include a variable called *friendliness* that represents friendly and polite discussion behavior. None of these would ultimately result in thread resolution if the answers that are offered were not targeted to the problems raised by the students who initiated the threads. This is one place where our work is very aligned with earlier work on QA sites. And thus we adopt a similar practice where we include in our model an estimate of answer appropriateness in a latent variable we refer to as *content matching*.

Now we define important terms used in our discussion. First, we define roles within discussion threads that are relevant for our work. For a given thread, the user who initialized the thread is called the **Starter**; the teaching staff including both official course instructors and TAs are referred to as **Instructors**; and any other users who have replied or commented in the thread are referred to as **Participants**. We count a thread in our dataset as **resolved** only if the thread starter personally changes the Unresolved button to Resolved. Otherwise, we count the as **unresolved**.

We are interested in the conditions under which a thread is marked as resolved or unresolved:

Thread Resolveability: Given a thread with its associated question and set of replies, which may not have been explicitly marked as resolved, identify whether it should have been marked as resolved or not.

4 Latent Variable Modeling

We laid the foundation for a conceptual model above to understand the factors associated with resolved versus unresolved threads and introduced five latent factors we referred to as Starter Influence, Expert Participation, Thread Popularity, Friendliness, and Content Matching. In this section, we further formalize these latent factors by specifying associated sets of observed variables that will ultimately enable us to evaluate our conceptual model. All latent and observed variables are enumerated in Table 1.

4.1 Starter Influence

The person who serves as the Thread starter is responsible for formulating the question that is addressed, and therefore the focus of that discussion. Some participants post many questions and are very adept at formulating their questions in ways that engage the attention of people who have the ability to provide answers. If the starter posts a lot and his/her questions often get resolved, this can be taken as an indication that this person is popular. Questions contributed by him/her may be more likely to attract attention and receive replies. This simple indication of popularity, which can be easily computed, may in some way compensate for the lack of an established badge system where they are not in use. We propose to measure this form of user influence by using the following four indicators. (1) Question Devotee x_{Pst}, indicates how many threads this question starter has proposed in this forum. Based on Figure 1(a), we divide users in this discussion forum into four types to indicate the propensity to post, i.e. post number ranges from 1-2 as standbys, 3-5 as less active, 6-14 as active, 40-489 as superstars. Similar partition method is adopted for all the following indicators. (2) Reply Devotee x_{Rep}, means how many times a person acts as a *Participant* in a thread posted by other students as shown in Figure 1(b). If he/she usually replies to others, then it is possible that his/her question will be paid more attention in return. (3) Resolved Favor x_{Res}, means in how many threads the person acts as the *Starter* in threads that get resolved. (4) Praised Responder x_{Uvt}, indicates the proportion of all the posts this starter makes in the forum that received upvotes, as displayed in Figure 1(d). This connects to how others recognize this starter and to what degree.

4.2 Expert Participation

Who participates a discussion is as important as who initiates the discussion. Students with some expertise in the related content can often provide quality replies (Anderson et al., 2012). Since user reputation score information is not available in this MOOC, it is necessary to for us to identify observable indicators. We define a person as Expert x_{Exp} in our forum as follows. A person is an Expert if and only if he/she is one of the instructors or his/her reputation score as we compute it is ranked in the top 1% among all students. The reputation score of student u is computed based on his/her question devotee u_{Pst}, reply devotee u_{Rep}, resolved favor u_{Res}, and praised recognition u_{Uvt} as we defined in the previous section. The contribution of each factor to reputation score is controlled using parameters α, β, γ.

$$\begin{aligned} score(u) =& \alpha u_{Pst} + \beta u_{Rep} + \gamma u_{Res} \\ &+ (1 - \alpha - \beta - \gamma) u_{Uvt} \end{aligned} \quad (1)$$

4.3 Thread Popularity

How much attention is paid to a question may be linked to the attractiveness of the thread based on how it is presented to the community. Thus modeling thread popularity may be valuable for accounting for variation in level of participation across threads. In particular, a reply is given upvotes when others think it is informative or good. Thus upvotes could indicate how others evaluate the replies in connection with the question. We design three observable factors here that may contribute to a model of thread popularity. The *Total UpVotes* x_{Tvt} and *Max UpVotes* x_{Mvt} are used to represent the credit this thread has received and how others recognize the current discussion. Based on our analysis, people rarely give a downvote to others' posts. The *Question Votes* x_{Svt} indicates whether the starter formulates a problem that wins recognition from others. For Total Upvotes, we find that in resolved threads, it is 6.10 compared to 3.15 in unresolved thread. Thus, intuitively, thread popularity has the potential to give a useful prediction of thread resolveability.

4.4 Friendliness

Friendliness (Danescu-Niculescu-Mizil et al., 2013; Burke and Kraut, 2008) concerns whether the current conversation is conducive for others to discuss ideas. This has not been considered in existing question answering work, and we thus discuss our operationalization of politeness here. We hypothesize that resolved threads posses more polite words, such as 'thank'. For example, a resolved thread might end with gratitude to thank others for providing help, and indeed we see this. Thus, we specify a set of observed indicators that may be useful in a latent variable model of politeness. (1) *Start with Thanks*: x_{Stx},

Var	T	Description	Var	T	Description	Var	T	Description
Pae	N	Please Count	Qa1	N	1st Match Score	Svt	N	Question Votes
Thx	N	Thanks Count	Qa2	N	2nd Match Score	Mvt	N	Max Votes
Dfe	N	Deference	Qa3	N	3rd Match Score	Uvt	N	User Votes
Etx	B	End with Thx	Len	N	Max Length	Rep	N	Reply Number
Stx	B	Start with Thx	Sim	N	Similarity	Res	N	Resolved Count
Exp	B	Expert Join	Tvt	N	Total Votes	Pst	N	Post Number
Sin	-	Starter Influence	Epr	-	Expert Participation	Con	-	Content Matching
Pop	-	Thread Popularity	Fen	-	Friendliness	Label	B	Resolved or not

Table 1: Variables used in the Structural Equation Model (SEM). Var is the factor variable that is used, which also corresponds to Figure 2. T indicates what type of values a variable can take. B is short for Binary. N is short for Numeric. '-' means it is a latent unobserved variable.

indicates whether this starter shows politeness when he/she posted the question. (2) *End with Thanks*: x_{Eth}, stands for whether the starter says thanks after receiving others' help. (3) *Thanks Count*: x_{Thx}, measures overall friendliness in the current discussion. We evaluate this by counting the thanking related words. (4) *Deference*: x_{Dfe}, is a count of positive polite words occurring in the discussion, such as using the words 'Nice','Great', or 'Awesome', as in prior work (Danescu-Niculescu-Mizil et al., 2013). Such words are used as markers to conduct counting. (5) *Please*: x_{Pae}, captures whether friendly question asking words were used, i.e. how many times words such as 'Please', 'Will', occur in current conversation.

4.5 Content Matching

Matches between the content of a thread and its replies indicate whether replies are relevant to answering the question instead of some off-topic discussion. In order to estimate this, we build an Eigenword bipartite graph to capture semantic similarities. Each node in the bipartite graph is the corresponding Eigenword[3] of a given word, with the left side representing the words that occurred in the thread starter, and the right side representing the words in a given reply. The edge is a similarity score computed by using the cosine similarity metric. In order to better identify whether a reply is discussing the content of the question, a semantic match between the thread question and its replies is needed. The top 3 matching scores are denoted as $x_{Qa1}, x_{Qa2}, x_{Qa3}$. Additionally, TF-IDF similarity x_{Sim} is computed (the correlation between x_{Sim} and $Qa1, Qa2, Qa3$ are $0.3280, 0.3572, 0.3569$ separately) and the maximum answer length x_{Len} is used to assist in computing the matching score.

[3]http://www.cis.upenn.edu/ ungar/eigenwords/

5 Experimental Investigation

In the above section, we described five latent factors we hypothesize are important in distinguishing resolved and unresolved threads along with sets of associated observed variables. In this section, we conduct two studies on thread resolveability, including validating the influence of each latent factor on thread resolution using a Structural Equation Model (SEM), and evaluating the generality of the identification of the resolveability using a predictive model. Experiments are conducted on the Python dataset with performance measurement under different evaluation metrics.

5.1 Conceptual SEM Validation

Our conceptual model is implemented as a Structural Equation Model (SEM) and is introduced as an evaluations of the effect of each latent factor on thread resolveability, as shown in Figure 2.

5.1.1 Conceptual SEM Model

A Structural Equation Model (Bollen, 1987), is a statistical technique for testing and estimating correlational (and sometimes causal) relations in cross sectional datasets. To explore the influence of our five latent factors, we take advantage of SEM to formalize the conceptual structure in order to measure what contributes to thread resolveability. The designed latent factors are specified as latent variables within the model, with the associated observed variables discussed above. We define the conceptual structure of how a thread gets resolved as well as a mathematical expression of each latent variable in Equation 2.

Related variables are explained above and

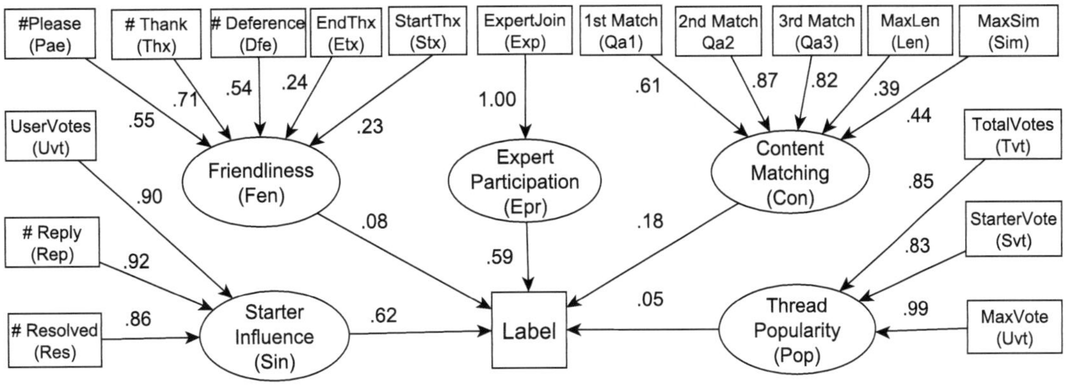

Figure 2: SEM Model Factor Analysis Result. Each directed edge indicates the predictive relationship. Weight on each directed edge is the estimated influence strength of one node to another. Table 1 illustrates the denotation. Only significant node influences whose p-value ($p < 0.05$) are presented. Circles stand for latent variables while rectangles signify observed variable.

summarized in Table 1. *Label* refers to the label of a unknown thread, taking the value of Resolved or Unresolved. *Label* (L) is a linear combination of each latent factor set. For each variable in a latent factor set, it is associated with a weight parameter γ in the SEM. Specifically, this conceptual structure of how a thread gets resolved relates to five aspects, i.e. (1) whether the thread starter has enough influence on others, (2) whether the relevant experts participated at least once in the discussion, (3) whether the thread polite and conducive to encouraging others to be willing to provide help, (4) whether the thread is popular, and (5) whether replies aim at answering questions instead of off topic discussion.

$$
\begin{aligned}
Con &= \gamma_{ci} \sum_{i=1}^{3} x_{Qai} + \gamma_{c4} x_{Sim} + \gamma_{c5} x_{Len} \\
Fen &= \gamma_{p1} x_{Stx} + \gamma_{p2} x_{Etx} + \gamma_{p3} x_{Thx} \\
&\quad + \gamma_{p4} x_{Dfe} + \gamma_{p5} x_{Pae} \\
Sin &= \gamma_{u1} x_{Rep} + \gamma_{u2} x_{Pst} + \gamma_{u3} x_{Res} + \gamma_{u4} x_{Uvt} \\
Pop &= \gamma_{t1} x_{Cmt} + \gamma_{t2} x_{Tvt} + \gamma_{t3} x_{Mvt} + \gamma_{t4} x_{Svt} \\
Epr &= \gamma_{a0} x_{Exp} \\
Label &= \zeta_1 Con + \zeta_2 Fen + \zeta_3 Sin \\
&\quad + \zeta_4 Pop + \zeta_5 Epr
\end{aligned} \tag{2}
$$

5.1.2 SEM Result Analysis

In this section, we discuss what we learn from the SEM about the influence of each factor within the model. We adopt the Structural Equation Model in R (Rosseel, 2012) to conduct the validation, and evaluate it by looking at the Comparative Fit Index (CFI), Root Mean Square Error of Approximation (RMSEA) and Standardized Root Mean Square Residual (SRMR) (Barrett, 2007). Figure 2 shows the influence of each observed variable on its corresponding latent variable, and in turn the latent variable on the resolved label. The weights on each directed edge represent the standard estimated parameter for measuring the influence. For the model fitting, we get a RMSEA of 0.09 and SRMR of 0.06, with a CFI of 0.89. The fit is not extremely high, but it is moderate, and it is within the range one would expect from a good fitting model when a large set of variables is considered.

Based on Figure 2, firstly, starter influence and expert participation contribute a lot to thread resolveability, with a standard estimated parameter of 0.619 and 0.587. This makes sense that who posts the question and who gives replies matter a lot in identifying whether a thread is resolved. Next, content matching contributes 0.178 to the resolving of a thread, which means matching between question and replies does differentiate between resolved and unresolved threads, but less so than who participates, perhaps because the observed variables are very shallow indicators of relevance. Friendliness is not very strongly predictive of resolvability. Similarly, Thread popularity contributes only 0.051 to the prediction, without significant influence compared to the other four latent variables, which are all significant. Thus we conclude that starter influence, expert participation, and content matching are strong factors while friendliness and thread popularity could help us separate resolved and unresolved threads, but less so than the other two.

5.2 Resolveability Prediction

The influences of five latent factors on thread resolveability are demonstrated as above. In this part, we build an ensemble logistic regression model to leverage those findings to predict whether a given thread is resolved or not.

5.2.1 Ensemble Regression Model

An ensemble logistic regression model is proposed to deal with the prediction of whether a thread is resolved or not. That is, given the question and a set of potential replies, as well as the five latent variables and associated observed variables, we want to predict whether a question has been answered. Our ensemble logistic model works in the following way. Firstly we train a separate logistic model for each of the five aspects defined above, i.e. five sub logistic model of how each aspect predicts the resolved property. Then those sub-models are included together in an ensemble in order to contribute to a final logistic model, which takes those results as the input features. Similar to generalized boosting (Friedman et al., 1998), this regression model integrates five weak predictors that capture five different aspects of thread resolveability, and construct a two layer logistic ensemble, which is distinct from a linear voting strategy. Our ensemble model relaxes the assumption of linearity and thus offers more flexibility in finding an effective predictive model. This process is formalized below.

$$\ddot{R}_j = \frac{1}{1 + e^{-\sum_{i=1}^{k} \alpha_i \cdot \dot{R}_{ij}}} \tag{3}$$

Here, k refers to the number of latent aspects. $\ddot{R}_j$ is the predicted resolved score for thread j; if it is larger than a threshold, the prediction of that thread question is resolved, otherwise it remains unresolved. $\dot{R}_{ij}$ is the predicted resolved score of latent factor set i on thread j, trained on the corresponding latent factor set.

5.2.2 Prediction Results

To demonstrate the predictive abilities of the five latent factors, we use our ensemble regression model to predict thread resolution. 10-fold cross validation is used, and the prediction results will be evaluated using the metrics Recall, Precision, and AUC (Area under Curve). For baselines, we begin with the simplest model **EndThx**, which simply bases the prediction on whether the current thread ends up with a gratitude sentence. This makes sense because it is natural that students will express their gratitude after receiving others' help. One simple baseline is the **Majority**, which predicts the testing thread as the majority status (unresolved in our dataset), leading to a accuracy of 0.503; **Si+Ep** is a combination of the latent aspect of starter influence and expert participation; and **Si+Ep+Ct** adds the content matching latent set on **Si+Ep**; **Si+Ep+Ct+Fr** is defined similarly. **ALL-Linear** is adding all five latent factor sets and predicts the resolved or not using a linear logistic regression. Comparably, **ALL-Ensemble** is trained using the nonlinear ensemble logistic regression model. The combination results as well as a comparison are summarized in Table 3. For the influence of each single latent aspect on the same prediction task, we present them correspondingly in Table 2, where Si, Ep, Ct, Tp, and Fr represent Student Influence, Expert Participation, Content Matching, Thread Populratiy, and Friendliness respectively.

Single Model	Precision	Recall	AUC
Si	0.697	0.696	0.791
Ep	0.602	0.590	0.572
Ct	0.626	0.616	0.647
Tp	0.594	0.579	0.626
Fr	0.639	0.633	0.685

Table 2: Prediction Result of Single Latent Factor

Model	Precision	Recall	AUC
EndThx	0.629	0.612	0.593
Si + Ep	0.803	0.802	0.857
Si+Ep+Ct	0.819	0.815	0.884
Si+Ep+Ct+Fr	0.823	0.823	0.893
ALL-Linear	0.826	0.826	0.894
ALL-Ensemble	**0.831**	**0.831**	**0.896**

Table 3: Prediction Result

Looking at the five latent aspects, (1) we conclude that, starter influence has the most powerful influence on thread resolution. It improves a lot on the Precision metric, and 50.25% on AUC compared to the **EndThx**. It makes sense that, if a user posts a lot, and often helps answer others' questions, it is more likely that his/her question will get a lot attention; (2) Thread Popularity, by itself works better than the baseline under the metric of AUC. The features in this set are not so directly connected to thread resolution from a conceptual standpoint compared to whether a thread ends with thanks. However, it unexpectedly achieves an AUC of 0.626, which is higher than the baseline. (3) For content matching, the precision is similar to that of **EndThx**, but in contrast, this model achieves a good improvement on AUC. Content matching describes the similarities between a question and a reply, which is a direct indication of whether the reply is trying to answer the question. (4) Friendliness has a significant predictive ability in connection with thread resolution. For the AUC, it offers about a 13% improvement over the baseline. It is reasonable that a resolved thread tends to be more polite, which means people use 'please', 'thanks' more than in other unresolved threads.

To build the ensemble models, we combine the latent factor sets in the order of their strength of estimated influence on resolveability. We firstly integrate the starter influence and expert participation, as we can see, it achieves significant improvement over the simpler baselines, with 28% higher on Precision, 31% on Recall and 45% on AUC. It even performs better on the three metrics than any of the single models in Table2. **Si+Ep+Ct** also gives a substantial increase on the metrics and when adding semantic content matching, **Si+Ep+Ct+Fr** is about 3% better than **Si+Ep** on precision and recall. This indicates that friendliness and content matching are capturing different aspects of the thread resolveability from starter influence and expert participation. Besides, the **ALL-Linear** performs best among all one layer regression models. This shows that even though thread popularity contributes least to resolved or not based on the SEM result, it gives a different perspective of the thread resolveability and is not to be ignored. When we applied our proposed ensemble regression model **ALL-Ensemble** using the five latent factor sets, we find that it outperforms all one layer logistic regressors, especially in Recall and Precision. This demonstrates that the two-layer ensemble logistic regression model's added representational power is needed for this problem.

6 Conclusions and Future Research

In this paper, we have focused on improving the thread resolveability in MOOC discussion forums. Our investigation is divided into two separate studies that leverage a common conceptual model involving five latent factors that are associated with thread resolution. Our first study validates the five latent variable structures using a SEM model, which helps us to validate our assumptions and hone in on those factors that are most promising to leverage in subsequent work. It enables us to assess the relative strength of each factor's influence on thread resolveability, and provides a foundation for the other study. The second study's focus is predicting thread resolution based on the first phase's findings. In addition to serving as a test of generality from trained data to unseen data, the predictive model may also have a practical benefit. In particular, thread resoveability identification could provide the potential to achieve a better allocation of valuable human resources to work on unresolved threads, which increases the potential for students to get their support needs met in Massive Open Online Courses. Our work is contenxtualized in the specifics of MOOCs as an online context including the particulars of interaction practices within those contexts. Thus, in addition to building on existing QA work in our feature engineering, we also introduce new directions, such as the linguistic modeling of speaker politeness, and conduct forms of latent semantic matching that have proven effective in dialogue systems.

However, we believe there is a need for further modeling in order to fully understand thread resolveability. A limitation of the current work is that it was conducted in only one course. Thus, we will be in a stronger position for moving forward if we explicitly address the question of generalizability across courses with further corpus based investigation. Besides, how to transfer the prediction models from forums with resolved buttons to ones that have no such affordances, which may be challenging because of differences in the distribution of behaviors.

Acknowledgement

This research was funded in part by NSF grants IIS-1320064 and OMA-0836012 and funding from Google.

References

Eugene Agichtein, Carlos Castillo, Debora Donato, Aristides Gionis, and Gilad Mishne. 2008. Finding high-quality content in social media. In *Proceedings of the 2008 International Conference on Web Search and Data Mining*, WSDM '08, pages 183–194, New York, NY, USA. ACM.

Eugene Agichtein, Yandong Liu, and Jiang Bian. 2009. Modeling information-seeker satisfaction in community question answering. *ACM Trans. Knowl. Discov. Data*, 3(2):10:1–10:27, April.

Ashton Anderson, Daniel Huttenlocher, Jon Kleinberg, and Jure Leskovec. 2012. Discovering value from community activity on focused question answering sites: A case study of stack overflow. In *Proceedings of the 18th ACM SIGKDD International Conference on Knowledge Discovery and Data Mining*, KDD '12, pages 850–858, New York, NY, USA. ACM.

Girish Balakrishnan. 2013. Predicting student retention in massive open online courses using hidden markov models. Master's thesis, EECS Department, University of California, Berkeley, May.

Paul Barrett. 2007. Structural equation modelling: Adjudging model fit. *Personality and Individual Differences*, 42(5):815–824.

Kenneth A Bollen. 1987. Total, direct, and indirect effects in structural equation models. *Sociological methodology*, 17(1):37–69.

Eric Brill, Susan Dumais, and Michele Banko. 2002. An analysis of the askmsr question-answering system. In *Proceedings of the ACL-02 Conference on Empirical Methods in Natural Language Processing - Volume 10*, EMNLP '02, pages 257–264, Stroudsburg, PA, USA. Association for Computational Linguistics.

Moira Burke and Robert Kraut. 2008. Mind your ps and qs: The impact of politeness and rudeness in online communities. In *Proceedings of the 2008 ACM Conference on Computer Supported Cooperative Work*, CSCW '08, pages 281–284, New York, NY, USA. ACM.

Cristian Danescu-Niculescu-Mizil, Moritz Sudhof, Dan Jurafsky, Jure Leskovec, and Christopher Potts. 2013. A computational approach to politeness with application to social factors. In *ACL (1)*, pages 250–259.

Jerome Friedman, Trevor Hastie, and Robert Tibshirani. 1998. Additive logistic regression: a statistical view of boosting. *Annals of Statistics*, 28:2000.

Peter Jansen, Mihai Surdeanu, and Peter Clark. 2014. Discourse complements lexical semantics for non-factoid answer reranking. In *Proceedings of the 52nd Annual Meeting of the Association for Computational Linguistics*, ACL '13=4. Association for Computational Linguistics.

Jiwoon Jeon, W. Bruce Croft, Joon Ho Lee, and Soyeon Park. 2006. A framework to predict the quality of answers with non-textual features. In *Proceedings of the 29th Annual International ACM SIGIR Conference on Research and Development in Information Retrieval*, SIGIR '06, pages 228–235, New York, NY, USA. ACM.

Yutaka Kabutoya, Tomoharu Iwata, Hisako Shiohara, and Ko Fujimura. 2010. Effective question recommendation based on multiple features for question answering communities. In *ICWSM*.

René F Kizilcec, Chris Piech, and Emily Schneider. 2013. Deconstructing disengagement: analyzing learner subpopulations in massive open online courses. In *Proceedings of the Third International Conference on Learning Analytics and Knowledge*, pages 170–179. ACM.

Ann Lieberman. 1995. Practices that support teacher development: Transforming conceptions of professional learning. *Innovating and Evaluating Science Education: NSF Evaluation Forums, 1992-94*, page 67.

Yandong Liu and Eugene Agichtein. 2008. You've got answers: Towards personalized models for predicting success in community question answering. In *Proceedings of the 46th Annual Meeting of the Association for Computational Linguistics on Human Language Technologies: Short Papers*, HLT-Short '08, pages 97–100, Stroudsburg, PA, USA. Association for Computational Linguistics.

Qiaoling Liu, Eugene Agichtein, Gideon Dror, Evgeniy Gabrilovich, Yoelle Maarek, Dan Pelleg, and Idan Szpektor. 2011. Predicting web searcher satisfaction with existing community-based answers. In *Proceedings of the 34th International ACM SIGIR Conference on Research and Development in Information Retrieval*, SIGIR '11, pages 415–424, New York, NY, USA. ACM.

Rivindu Perera. 2012. Ipedagogy: Question answering system based on web information clustering. In *Technology for Education (T4E), 2012 IEEE Fourth International Conference on*, pages 245–246. IEEE.

Chris Piech, Jonathan Huang, Zhenghao Chen, Chuong Do, Andrew Ng, and Daphne Koller. 2013. Tuned models of peer assessment in MOOCs. In *Proceedings of The 6th International Conference on Educational Data Mining (EDM 2013)*.

John Prager, Eric Brown, Anni Coden, and Dragomir Radev. 2000. Question-answering by predictive annotation. In *Proceedings of the 23rd Annual International ACM SIGIR Conference on Research and Development in Information Retrieval*, SIGIR '00, pages 184–191, New York, NY, USA. ACM.

Mingcheng Qu, Guang Qiu, Xiaofei He, Cheng Zhang, Hao Wu, Jiajun Bu, and Chun Chen. 2009. Probabilistic question recommendation for question answering communities. In *Proceedings of the 18th International Conference on World Wide Web*, WWW '09, pages 1229–1230, New York, NY, USA. ACM.

Carolyn Penstein Rosé, Ryan Carlson, Diyi Yang, Miaomiao Wen, Lauren Resnick, Pam Goldman, and Jennifer Sherer. 2014. Social factors that contribute to attrition in moocs. In *Proceedings of the first ACM conference on Learning@ scale conference*, pages 197–198. ACM.

Yves Rosseel. 2012. lavaan: An r package for structural equation modeling. *Journal of Statistical Software*, 48(2):1–36, 5.

Chirag Shah and Jefferey Pomerantz. 2010. Evaluating and predicting answer quality in community qa. In *Proceedings of the 33rd International ACM SIGIR Conference on Research and Development in Information Retrieval*, SIGIR '10, pages 411–418, New York, NY, USA. ACM.

Juyup Sung, Jae-Gil Lee, and Uichin Lee. 2013. Booming up the long tails: Discovering potentially contributive users in community-based question answering services. In *ICWSM*.

Qiongjie Tian, Peng Zhang, and Baoxin Li. 2013. Towards predicting the best answers in community-based question-answering services. In Emre Kiciman, Nicole B. Ellison, Bernie Hogan, Paul Resnick, and Ian Soboroff, editors, *ICWSM*. The AAAI Press.

Miaomiao Wen, Diyi Yang, and Carolyn Penstein Rosé. 2014. Linguistic reflections of student engagement in massive open online courses. In *Proceedings of the International Conference on Weblogs and Social Media*.

Diyi Yang, Tanmay Sinha, David Adamson, and Carolyn Penstein Rose. 2013. turn on, tune in, drop out: Anticipating student dropouts in massive open online courses. In *Workshop on Data Driven Education, Advances in Neural Information Processing Systems 2013*.

Diyi Yang, Miaomiao Wen, and Carolyn Rose. 2014. Peer influence on attrition in massive open online courses. In *Proceedings of Educational Data Mining*.

Wen-tau Yih, Ming-Wei Chang, Christopher Meek, and Andrzej Pastusiak. 2013. Question answering using enhanced lexical semantic models. In *Proceedings of the 51st Annual Meeting of the Association for Computational Linguistics (Volume 1: Long Papers)*, pages 1744–1753, Sofia, Bulgaria, August. Association for Computational Linguistics.

Point-of-View Mining and Cognitive Presence in MOOCs: A (Computational) Linguistics Perspective

Noureddine Elouazizi
Science Center for Learning and Teaching, University of British Columbia
Center for Teaching and Learning Technologies, University of British Columbia
Department of Linguistics, Simon Fraser University
Vancouver, British Columbia
Email: noureddine.elouazizi@ubc.ca

Abstract

This paper explores the cognitive presence of the learners in MOOCs through using a (computational) linguistic analysis of the learners' Point-of-View as an indicator for cognitive presence. The linguistic analysis of the written language as a medium of interaction by the students in the context of MOOCs shows hallmarks of cognitive disengagement and low cognitive presence by the learners.

1. Introduction

The popularity of Massive Open Online Courses (henceforth MOOCs) is expanding, and the perceived educational add-value of their scalability to the masses is growing. However, research shows that MOOCs do not generate enough opportunities for students' interaction and retention (see: Kizilcec *et al* (2013), Yang *et al* (2013), Rosé *et al* (2014), Wen *et al* (2014b). The large scale linguistic data that is generated by discussion boards, blogs, and other written language-based interaction tools that are/can be part of the MOOC technology infrastructure provides an unprecedented opportunity to study the dynamics of students' interaction, learning engagement, and ways in which critical valuable learning/teaching discourse is constructed around different knowledge topics.

This paper presents an exploratory approach to examine students' learning-based inquiry within the context of MOOCs through analyzing the linguistic aspects of Point-of-View as an indicator of cognitive presence. This approach is theoretically grounded in linguistics (natural syntax) and educationally understood along the lines of the Community of Inquiry Framework (Garrison *et al* (2000), Garrison *et al* (2001), Swan *et al* (2009)).

2. Background

2.1. Point-of-View: a linguistics perspective

I assume that the structure and the interpretation of Point-of-View as a linguistic construct is detected and interpreted through its compositional parts. The compositional parts of Point-of-View include notions such as: *subjectivity, belief mitigation, evidentiality* and *epistemic mood* (Speas and Tenny 2003, Elouazizi 2014). The notion of subjectivity refers to the way a speaker expresses knowledge gained through personal/internal experience-"ontological subjectivity" (Searle 2004). The notion of (belief) mitigation is linguistically conveyed through the use of a specific set of epistemic parenthetical verbs such as: *think, believe* (Urmson (1952)).

In addition to the use of belief mitigation verbs, and subjectivity linguistic devices, a speaker's point of view is also indicated by the degree of their use of evidential verbs that carry epistemic propositional attitudes, such as: *I feel, I sense, I see*. A subject/speaker uses evidentiality linguistic devices (verbs, adverbs) to evaluate the degree of certainty in a proposition by matching the source of the information and the target of the information (Speas 2008).

In addition to these linguistic devices, Point-of-View can also be conveyed through the use of a set of epistemic mood and discourse adverbs. This includes adverbs such as: *frankly, presumably, supposedly, probably, luckily, realistically*. These adverbs provide additional information about the propositional attitude of the speaker.

Taken jointly, the combination of these linguistic constructs constitutes a lexical structure (lexicon), with a latent syntax of Point-of-View, and which can lend itself to the techniques of text mining and computational linguistic analysis.

Proceedings of the 2014 Conference on Empirical Methods in Natural Language Processing (EMNLP), pages 32–37,
October 25-29, 2014, Doha, Qatar.

2.2. Point-of-View: a learning perspective

Defined in broad terms, learning events are the set of "*activities*" and "*acts*" that the learner engages in so as to ensure the acquisition, transfer and modification of knowledge, skills and beliefs (Skinner (1968), Piaget (1952), Gagné (1985), Mayer (1996)). These (learning) activities and acts could be internal (mental) or/and external (behaviours) and could include more than one cognitive modality for processing information. These modalities include: auditory modality, visual modality, haptic modality, and linguistic modality. Each of these cognitive modalities produces data (information) that can be studied to infer whether and how learning occurs.

My focus here is on the linguistic modality, and how it is used to interface the components of an educational/learning experience, as understood within the context of the Community of Inquiry model for learning (see: Garrison *et al* (2000) and Garrison *et al* (2001)). Perceived from the perspective of the Community of Inquiry (CoI) model, I propose that the analysis of Point-of-View is a way to examine the nature of the supporting discourse that is crucial in interfacing the *social presence*, the *cognitive presence*, and the *teaching presence* (as illustrated in the adapted Figure in 1).

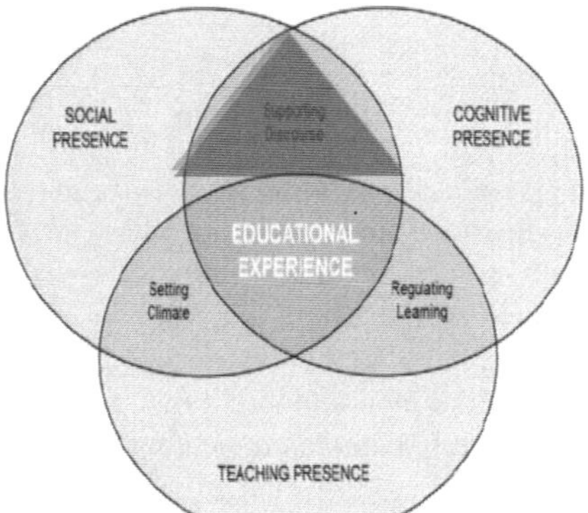

FIGURE 1: Community of Inquiry (CoI) model (Adapted from: Garrison *et al* 2000)

One of the central aspects of CoI is "cognitive presence". This refers to the "extent to which the participating learners in any particular configuration of a community of inquiry are able to construct meaning through sustained communication." (Garrison *et al*, Swan *et al* (2009)). I explore the cognitive presence of the MOOC's learners through the analysis of Point-of-View's usage, clustering and dispersions in the written language-based interactions, generated by the learners in the context of MOOCs.

3. Method

3.1. Data sets: the corpus

This paper uses two data sets of written language corpus. The first data set is from the blogs discussions of three MOOC courses, attended by 3000 learners, and English language was the language of interaction in these MOOCs. The second set of data comes from the discussion board of a large online university course, delivered to a large class of 300 students, using English language. The written corpus data from the three MOOCs contains 724955 words, and the corpus data from the non-MOOC online course contains 727205 words.

Lexical & Referential density	Three MOOCs	One online course
Words in data set	724955	727205
Lexical density: Lexemes per data set	475064	381392
Lexical density: Lexemes %	61.17%	52.91%
Reference density: 1st Person (speaker)	2.32%	2.98%
Reference density: 2nd Person (hearer)	0.95%	0.16
# of learners	3000	300

TABLE 1: *lexical and referential density in the data sets*

The data in table 1 was generated from the MOOC and the non-MOOC corpus data, using the corpus tool Systemic coder (available at: http://www.wagsoft.com/CorpusTool).

3.2. Point-of-View extraction: the approach

One central non-trivial challenge with the computational extraction of the linguistic patterns from written text is the issue of *classification* and *feature structures*. The term classification is generally construed broadly to encompass the architecture and the structure of the systems and features used in extracting interpretative patterns such as opinions and sentiments from written text (Riloff and Wiebe (2003), Pang and Lee (2004)). There are different approaches to extraction to guide the computational process of automatically extracting patterns from text.

For example, the approach of *polarity-based classification* encompasses regression and ranking of the lexical units. This approach is exploited in sentiment analysis and it assumes that the text is underlined by an opinion towards which an agent expresses a positive or negative feeling (see: Pang *et al.* (2002), Eguchi and Lavrenko (2006)).

Another approach is the *gradability-based classification*. In this approach the lexical units are not attributed a polar classification. Rather, the text is classified in terms of gradable terms. This approach is used in automatic extraction of *subjectivity* from the text (Wiebe *et al.* (2001), Wilson *et al.* (2005), Yu and Hatzivassiloglou (2003)).

I build on the insights of *polarity-based* and *gradability-based* approaches to automatic extraction and processing of text and propose the classification in Figure 2.

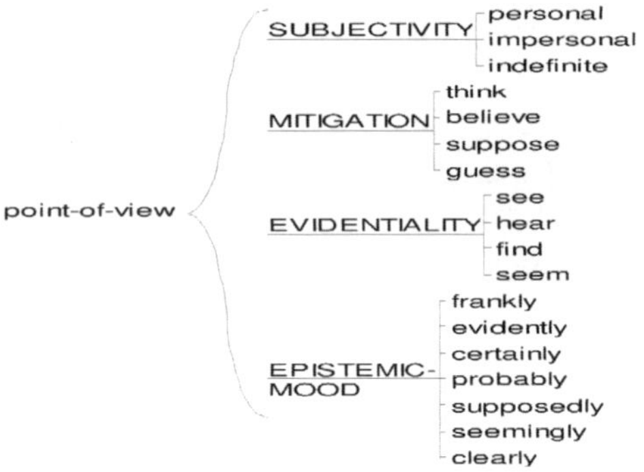

FIGURE 2: *The classification features structure of Point-of-View*

The classification and features structure in Figure 2 enables the extraction of a bundle of attitudes and belief as it uses a combination of parts of speech that encompass latent knowledge and interpretations, as exhibited in the syntax and the semantics of the constructs that compose Point-of-View. As such, Point-of-View mining and automatic analysis is at the intersection of opinion mining and subjectivity mining. This approach (Point-of-View mining) seeks to extract perspective-related information such as opinion holders, belief mitigation, and propositional attitudes (for similar but not identical approaches, see: Kudo and Matsumoto (2004), Dave *et al* (2003), Riloff and Wiebe (2003), Song *et al* 2007, El-Halees (2011)).

4. Results and discussion

Recall that the main goal of this paper is to explore the cognitive presence of the learners in MOOCs through their written language input, and using a linguistics analysis of the learners' Point-of-View as an indicator for cognitive presence. I hypothesize that if the learners in MOOCs are cognitively disengaged, the frequency and usage of Point-of-View components (as identified in Figure 2) would be low. Conversely, if the frequency and usage of Point-of-View components is higher, that would imply that the students in MOOCs are cognitively engaged and their cognitive presence is more asserted.

The Point-of-View usage data, as illustrated in FIGURE 3, shows that the use of belief mitigation devices (verbs such as: *think, believe, guess* and *suppose*) is equally low in all the three MOOCs.

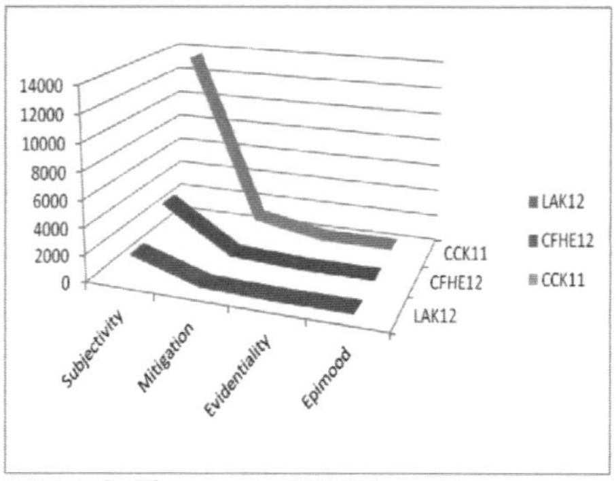

FIGURE 3: *The usage of POV/cognitive presence in MOOCs*

However, in all the three MOOCs, subjectivity is attested with varying degrees. This indicates that the learners do express their stance in their blog discussions but without engaging in any epistemic interactions with other learners. This is the case because the uses of the mitigation construct, of the evidentiality construct, and of the epistemic mood construct by a speaker (learner) always requires predicating on, hence interacting with previously mentioned/stated proposition. The data in Figure 3 indicates that the learners did not modify the propositions that were put forward by other learners or convey changes in propositional attitudes, or mitigate beliefs, expressed in the text of the MOOCs blogs.

These observations are further supported by the dispersion and clustering analysis of the data, as illustrated in Figure 4.

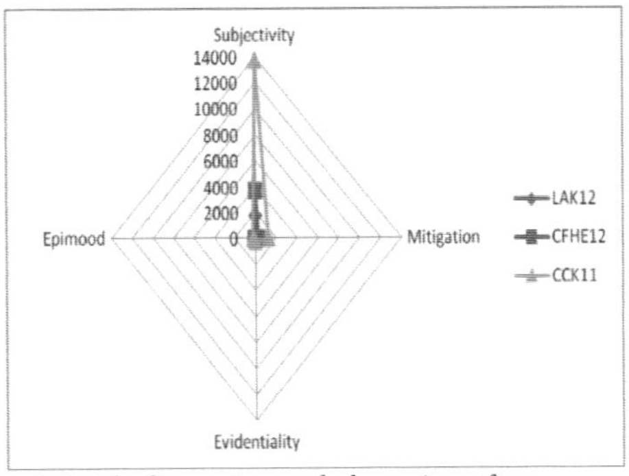

FIGURE 4: *dispersion and clustering of POV/cognitive presence in MOOCs*

Assuming that "support discourse" within the context of the CoI framework is crucial in interfacing the cognitive presence, the social presence and the teaching presence of the learner within an educational experience (see FIGURE 1 above), the use of written language as a medium of interaction by the students in the context of MOOCs shows hallmarks of cognitive disengagement and low cognitive presence. That this is indeed the case is further indicated by the Point-of-View comparative data that illustrates the use of Point-of-View in the context of a MOOC versus its use in the context of a non-MOOC online course.

Consider the differences in the Point-of-View usage, dispersion and clustering between the data set of a single MOOC ccourse and that of a non-MOOC online course, as illustrated by Figure 5 and Figure 6 below. The Point-of-View usage comparative data illustrated in Figure 5 indicates that the cognitive presence and engagement of the learners in the non-MOOC online course is significantly higher than in the MOOC courses.

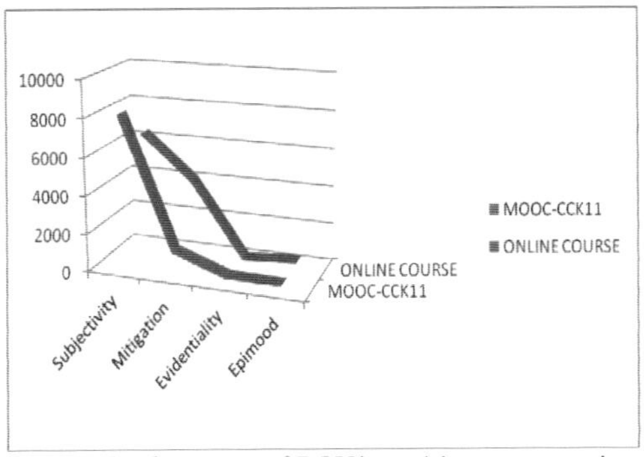

FIGURE 5: *The usage of POV/cognitive presence in a MOOC vs. non-MOOC online course*

The learners in the non-MOOC online course produced linguistic structures that contain speech acts of expressing subjective views, of mitigating aforementioned propositions (beliefs) in the discourse and of providing evidence of a statement as indicated through the use of evidential adverbs. However, the language (linguistic structures) used by the learners in a single MOOC course shows higher level of subjective use than the non-MOOC course but significantly lower usage of speech acts that express mitigation of beliefs or evidentiality.

Furthermore, the usage of the Point-of-View in the non-MOOC online course shows that the learners expressed higher subjectivity, accompanied with higher rates of belief mitigation. This suggests that the learners in the non-MOOC online course were more cognitively engaged and they actively engaged in invoking the discourse structures that support the interfacing of cognitive presence, teaching presence and social presence. These observations are further supported by the Point-of-View dispersion and clustering data represented in Figure 6.

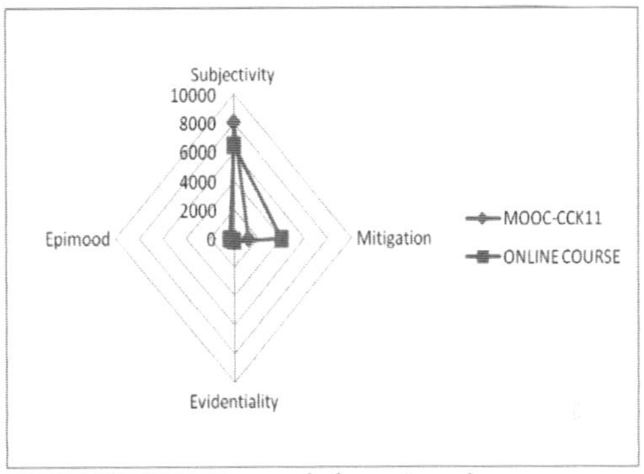

FIGURE 6: *dispersion and clustering of POV/cognitive presence in a MOOC vs. non-MOOC online course*

All in all, the data above indicates that learners within the context of MOOCs exhibit less cognitive presence than their counter part learners in a non-MOOC online course. The linguistic structures used by the learners in the context of a MOOC course, at least on the basis of the data examined in this paper, indicate that they did not mitigate and attach evidential statements to as many propositions as in a non-MOOC course. For a speaker to mitigate a proposition, the speaker first needs to be aware of the proposition, the agent who proposed or enacted such a proposition before mitigating it. Hence, the more a speaker mitigates hers or the propositions of others, the more the speaker is engaged with the discourse constructed around different knowledge topics.

These findings square with and confirm observations established in other studies which analyze the learners' engagement in MOOCs. For example, Wen *et al.* (2014a) and Wen *et al* (2014b), using a survival model, and drawing on linguistic data in discussion posts, show that learners' engagement in MOOCs reduces drastically after week three in a MOOC course.

5. Conclusion and future work

This paper explored the use of a computational linguistic perspective to mine and exploit the latent knowledge in the Point-of-View construct to examine the cognitive presence and engagement of the students in the context of MOOC and non-MOOC courses. As the results show, the linguistic analysis of the written language as a medium of interaction by the learners in the context of MOOCs shows hallmarks of cognitive disengagement and low cognitive presence by the learners.

However, what emerges in the context of this exploratory paper is a partial representation of the learning-based discourse structure within MOOCs and is by no means conclusive of the way discourse structures are constructed around different knowledge topics within the context of a MOOC vs. a non-MOOC online course. The empirical testing of the classification in Figure 2, from a text mining and automatic extraction perspective is yet to be validated on larger (fully) annotated MOOCs data sets, and using larger integrated lexicons that combine a Point-of-View latent knowledge lexicon and a MOOCs specific education experience lexicon.

Acknowledgments

I would like to thank Carolyn Penstein Rosé and George Siemens for sharing with me the MOOCs blog discussions data that I used as part of the data sets that this paper studies.

6. References

Dave, K., Lawrence, S., Pennock, D.M. 2003. Mining the peanut gallery: Opinion extraction and semantic classification of product reviews. In *Proceedings of WWW*, pages 519–528.

Elouazizi, Noureddine. 2014. *The formal syntax of point-of-view and belief mitigation*. PhD Dissertation, SFU.

El-Halees, A. 2011. Mining opinions in user-generated contents to improve course evaluation. In *Software Engineering and Computer Systems*, pages 107-115. Springer.

Eguchi, K and Lavrenko, V.2006. Sentiment retrieval using generative models. In *Proceedings of the Conference on Empirical Methods in Natural Language Processing (EMNLP)*, pages 345–354.

Gagné, R. M. 1985. *The conditions of learning* (4th ed.). New York: Holt, Rinehart & Winston.

Garrison, D. R., Anderson, T, & Archer, W. 2000. Critical inquiry in a text-based environment: Computer conferencing in higher education. *The Internet and Higher Education* 2: 87–105.

Garrison, D. R., Anderson, T., & Archer, W. 2001. Critical thinking, cognitive presence and computer conferencing in distance education. *American Journal of Distance Education,* 15(1), 7-23.

Kizilcec, R. F., Piech, C. and Schneider, E. 2013. Deconstructing disengagement: analyzing learner subpopulations in massive open online courses. In *Proceedings of the Third International Conference on Learning Analytics and Knowledge*, pages 170-179.ACM.

Kudo, T. and Matsumoto, Y. 2004. A boosting algorithm for classification of semi-structured text. In *Proceedings of the Conference on Empirical Methods in Natural Language Processing (EMNLP).*

Mayer, R. E. 1996. Learners as information processors: Legacies and limitations of educational psychology's second metaphor. *Educational Psychologist, 31,* 151–161.

Pang, B., Lee, L. and Vaithyanathan, S. 2002. Thumbs up? Sentiment classification using machine learning techniques. In *Proceedings of the Conference on Empirical Methods in Natural Language Processing (EMNLP)*, pages 79–86.

Pang, B. and Lee, L. 2004. A sentimental education: Sentiment analysis using subjectivity summarization based on minimum cuts. In *Proceedings of the Association for Computational Linguistics (ACL)*, pages 271–278.

Piaget, J.-P. 1952. *The origins of intelligence in children*. International Universities Press, New York.

Rosé, C. P., Carlson, R., Yang, D., Wen, M., Resnick, L., Goldman, P. & Sherer, J. 2014. Social Factors that Contribute to Attrition in MOOCs. In P*roceedings of the First ACM Conference on Learning @ Scale*(poster).

Swan, K., Garrison, D. R. & Richardson, J. C. 2009. A constructivist approach to online learning: the Community of Inquiry framework. In Payne, C. R. (Ed.) *Information Technology and Constructivism in Higher Education: Progressive Learning Frameworks*. Hershey, PA: IGI Global, 43-57.

Song, D., Lin, H. and Yang. Z. 2007. Opinion mining in e-learning system. In *Network and Parallel Computing Workshop*. IFIP International Conference , P.788-792. IEEE.

Searle, J. 2003. *Mind: a brief introduction*. Oxford University Press.

Speas, Peggy. (2008). On the Syntax and Semantics of Evidentials. *Language and Linguistics Compass*. Volume 2 Issue 5, pp. 940 – 965.

Speas, Peggy, and Tenny, Carol. 2003. Configurational Properties of Point of View Roles. In DiSciullo, A. (ed.), *Asymmetry in Grammar*. Amsterdam: John Benjamins. 315-344.

Urmson, J. O. 1952. Parenthetical verbs. *Mind*. 61. 480-496.

Wen, M., Yang, D., & Rosé, C. P. 2014a. Sentiment Analysis in MOOC Discussion Forums: What does it tell us? In *Proceedings of Educational Data Mining*.

Wen, M., Yang, D., & Rosé, C. P. 2014b. Linguistic Reflections of Student Engagement in Massive Open Online Courses. In *Proceedings of the International Conference on Weblogs and Social Media*.

Wiebe, J.M., Wilson, T and Bell, M. 2001. Identifying collocations for recognizing opinions. In *Proceedings of the ACL/EACL Workshop on Collocation: Computational Extraction, Analysis, and Exploitation*.

Wiebe, J. and Wilson, T. 2002. Learning to disambiguate potentially subjective expressions. In *Proceedings of the Conference on Natural Language Learning (CoNLL)*, pages 112–118.

Wiebe., J., Theresa W. M., Bruce, R., Bell, M., and Martin, M. 2004. Learning subjective language. *Computational Linguistics*, 30(3):277–308.

Wilson, T., Wiebe, J. Hoffmann, P. 2005. Recognizing contextual polarity in phrase-level sentiment analysis. In *Proceedings of the Human Language Technology Conference and the Conference on Empirical Methods in Natural Language Processing (HLT/EMNLP)*, pages 347–354.

Yang, D., Sinha, T., Adamson, D., & Rosé, C. P. 2013. Turn on, Tune in, Drop out: Anticipating student dropouts in Massive Open Online Courses. In *NIPS Data-Driven Education Workshop*.

Yu, H., Hatzivassiloglou, V. 2003. Towards answering opinion questions: Separating facts from opinions and identifying the polarity of opinion sentences. In *Proceedings of the Conference on Empirical Methods in Natural Language Processing (EMNLP)*.

Analytics: climbing up the ladder of behavior control

Patrick Jermann
Ecole Polytechnique Fédérale
de Lausanne
Station 20
CH-1015 Lausanne
Patrick.Jermann@epfl.ch

Abstract

Learning Analytics can be conceptualized as an action control process. Information is collected at the behavioral level and then re-mapped to serve diagnosis at higher levels of control. We describe the rationale for moving up the ladder of behavior control with examples from eye-tracking and clickstream analysis.

1 Overview

Sensors used in analytics collect data at low temporal resolutions. Eye-tracking systems for example record gaze at a very high rate (250 Hz) without semantic information. Similarly, clickstream data collected online represent atomic actions that do not reflect the orientation of the learner's behavior. On the opposite, the expected output of an analytics system should inform decision-making at a much higher level, for example, is a learner going to drop out of a course at the end of a week, or do partners understand each other. The gap between sensor data and indicators useful for decision requires the re-mapping of behavioral streams into cognitively meaningful indicators. The computation of indicators should ideally be content independent and calibration free.

We will describe the development of gaze indicators that reflect the breadth of the focus of attention and the coupling between a listener and a speaker. In dyadic interaction, these indicators are related to the level of abstraction of dialogue and the quality of interaction. We extended the rationale of these indicators to the case of one user listening to a video lecture with the notion of *with-me-ness*: similar to teachers wondering whether their students are "with them". Students who attend more closely to the references made by the teacher indeed achieve better learning.

An obvious limitation of gaze-based analytics is that eye-trackers are not (yet) widespread. We are investigating whether video-watching behavior captured by clickstream logs can serve as a proxy for attention. First results are encouraging and show that it is possible to define an information-processing index that reflects the engagement of learners with the video. This indicator is sensitive to both in video drop-out and course drop-out and reflects whether students process video superficially (speeding up, scrolling forward) or more intensively (checking back for reference, rewatching). Similar to the approach we followed for gaze re-mapping, we aggregate the atomic actions (Play, Pause, Seek back) into more meaningful actions that are psychologically more meaningful to assess learning strategies.

Proceedings of the 2014 Conference on Empirical Methods in Natural Language Processing (EMNLP), page 38,
October 25-29, 2014, Doha, Qatar.

Shared Task on Prediction of Dropout Over Time in Massively Open Online Courses

Carolyn P. Rosé
Language Technologies Institute
and Human-Computer Interaction Institute
Carnegie Mellon University
5000 Forbes Avenue, Pittsburgh, PA 15213
cprose@cs.cmu.edu

George Siemens
Center for Distributed Education
University of Texas at Arlington
701 South Nedderman Drive, Arlington, TX 76019
gsiemens@uta.edu

Abstract

The shared task on Prediction of Dropout Over Time in MOOCs involves analysis of data from 6 MOOCs offered through Coursera. Data from one MOOC with approximately 30K students was distributed as training data and consisted of discussion forum data (in SQL) and clickstream data (in JSON format). The prediction task was Predicting Attrition Over Time. Based on behavioral data from a week's worth of activity in a MOOC for a student, predict whether the student will cease to actively participate after that week. This paper describes the task. A full write up of the results is published separately (Rosé & Siemens, 2014).

1 Overview

Research on Massively Open Online Courses (MOOCs)[1] is an emerging area for real world impact of technology for analysis of social media at a large scale (Breslow et al., 2013). Modeling user experience in MOOCs supports research towards understanding user needs better so that experiences that are more conducive to learning can be offered. Beyond that, automated analyses enable adaptive technology to tailor the experience of users in real time (Rosé et al., 2014a). This paper describes a shared task designed to enlist the involvement of the language technologies community in this endeavor and to identify what value expertise within the field might bring.

[1] http://www.moocresearch.com/reports

One area for impact of natural language processing in the MOOC space is in modeling behavior within the threaded discussion forums. In a typical MOOC, between 5% and 10% of students actively participate in the threaded discussion forums. Previously published research demonstrates that characteristics of posting behavior are predictive of dropout along the way (Rosé et al., 2014b; Wen et al., 2014a; Wen et al., 2014b; Yang et al., 2013; Yang et al., 2014). However, ideally, we would like to make predictions for the other 90% to 95% of students who do not post. Thus, in this shared task, we challenge participants to use models of social interaction as displayed through the text-based interaction between students in the threaded discussions (from the minority of students who participate in them) to make meaning from the clickstream data we have from all students. If the discussion data can be thus leveraged to make more effective models of the clickstream data, then a meaningful prediction about drop out along the way can also be made about the students who do not post to the discussion forums.

One of the biggest challenges in the shared task is that the participants were only given data from one Coursera MOOC as training and development data. Their task was to produce a predictive model that could be applied to data from other MOOCs they did not have access to. A separate report describes a detailed analysis of the results applying submitted models to each of 5 test MOOCs (Rosé & Siemens, 2014).

12 research teams signed up for the shared task, including an international assortment of academic and industrial teams. Out of these 12 teams, only 4 submitted final models (Sinha et al., 2014; Sharkey & Sanders, 2014; Amnueypornsakul et al., 2014; Kloft et al., 2014).

In the remainder of this paper we describe the shared task in greater detail and discuss plans for future related research.

Proceedings of the 2014 Conference on Empirical Methods in Natural Language Processing (EMNLP), pages 39–41,
October 25-29, 2014, Doha, Qatar.

2 Shared Task

Participants in the shared task were given a complete SQL dump and clickstream dump from one Coursera MOOC as training data. The student-week was the unit of analysis. In other words, a prediction was made for each student for each week of their active participation to predict whether that week was the last week of their active participation. Scripts were provided to parse the data into a form that could be used for the task, e.g., aggregating entries per user per week. Scripts were also provided for running a test of the trained model on test data. The purpose of the scripts was to standardize the way in which each team's work would later be evaluated on the test MOOCs that participants did not have access to.

A major part of the work in doing the task is in determining what an effective representation would be of the behavior trace associated with each student-week that would enable making an accurate prediction. In other words, the question is what are the danger signs that a student is especially vulnerable to drop out? The rules of the task were such that the information the model was allowed to use for making the prediction could be extracted from the whole participation history of all training students (including both the SQL data and the clickstream data) up to and including the week a prediction was being made for.

Each of the four finalist teams submitted a final model trained on the training MOOC and a write up includeing result trained on a designated subset of students from the training MOOC and tested on the remaining students. Results were presented in terms of precision, recall, and fmeasure for the held out users.

We recommend that participants make use of the text data to bootstrap effective models that use only clickstream data. However, participants were welcome to leverage either type of data in the models they submitted. In our evaluation presented separately (Rosé & Siemens, 2014), we evaluated the models on the test MOOCs in three different ways: First, an evaluation was conducted on data from students who actively participated in the discussion forums. Second, an evaluation was conducted on data from students who never participated in the discussion forums. And finally, and evaluation was conducted on the set of students that includes both types of students.

Each submission consisted of a write up describing the technical approach and a link to a downloadable zip file containing the trained model and code and/or a script for using the trained model to make predictions about the test sets. The code was required to be runnable by launching a single script in Ubuntu 12.04. A code stub for streamlining the preparation of the submission was distributed with the data. The following programming languages were acceptable: R 3.1, C++ 4.7, Java 1.6, or Python 2.7. The script was required to be able to run within 24 hours on a 2400 MHz machine with 6 cores.

3 Looking Forward

Computational modeling of massive scale social interaction (as in MOOCs and other environments for learning at scale) has the potential to yield new knowledge about the inner-workings of interaction in such environments so that support for healthy community formation can be designed and built. However, the state-of-the-art in graphical models applied to large scale social data provides representations of the data that are challenging to interpret in light of specific questions that may be asked from a learning sciences or social psychological perspective. What is needed are new methodologies for development and interpretation of models that bridge expertise from machine learning and language technologies on one side and learning sciences, sociolinguistics, and social psychology on the other side. The field of language technologies has the human capital to take leadership in making these breakthroughs.

The shared task described in this paper is the first one like it where a data set from a Coursera MOOC has been made publically available so that a wide range of computational modeling techniques can be evaluated side by side (Rosé & Siemens, 2014). However, there is recognition that such shared tasks may play an important role in shaping the future of the field of Learning Analytics going forward (Pea, 2014).

One of the major challenges in running a shared task like this is ensuring the protection of privacy of the MOOC participants. Such concerns have been the focus of much discussion in the area of learning at scale (Asilomar Convention, 2014).

Data sharing ethics were carefully considered in the design of this shared task. In particular, all of the students who participated in the MOOC that produced the training data were told that their data would be used for research purposes. The data was carefully preprocessed to remove personal identifiers about the students and the university that hosted the course. All of the workshop participants who got access to the data were required to participate in human subjects training and to agree to use the data only for this workshop, and not to share it beyond their team. Data was shared through a secure web connection. Approval for use of the data in this fashion was approved by the Institutional Review Board of the hosting university as well as the university that ran the MOOC.

It was a goal in development of this shared task to serve as a forerunner in what we hope will become a more general practice of community wide collaboration on large scale learning analytics (Suthers et al., 2013).

Acknowledgements

The authors would like to thank Norman Bier for assistance in working through the data sharing logistics. This work was funded in part by NSF Grant OMA-0836012.

References

Amnueypornsakul, B., Bhat, S., & Chinprutthiwong, P. (2014). Predicting Attrition Along the Way: The UIUC Model, in *Proceedings of the 2014 Empirical Methods in Natural Language Processing Workshop on Modeling Large Scale Social Interaction in Massively Open Online Courses, Qatar, October 2014.*

Asilomar Convention (2014). *The Asilomar Convention for Learning Research in Higher Education*, June 13, 2014.

Breslow, L., Pritchard, D., De Boer, J., Stump, G., Ho, A., & Seaton, D. (2013). Studying Learning in the Worldwide Classroom : Research into edX's First MOOC, *Research & Practice in Assessment* (8).

Kloft, M., Stiehler, F., Zheng, Z., & Pinkward, N. (2014). Predicting MOOC Dropout over Weeks Using Machine Learning Methods, in *Proceedings of the 2014 Empirical Methods in Natural Language Processing Workshop on Modeling Large Scale Social Interaction in Massively Open Online Courses, Qatar, October 2014.*

Pea, R. (2014). *The Learning Analytics Workgroup: A Report on Building the Field of Learning Analytics for Personalized Learning at Scale*, Stanford University.

Rosé, C. P. & Siemens, G. (2014). *Shared Task Report : Results of the EMNLP 2014 Shared Task on Predictions of Dropout Over Time in MOOCs*, Langauge Technologies Institute Technical Report.

Rosé, C. P., Goldman, P., Sherer, J. Z., Resnick, L. (2014a). Supportive Technologies for Group Discussion in MOOCs, *Current Issues in Emerging eLearning*, Special issue on MOOCs, December 2014.

Rosé, C. P., Carlson, R., Yang, D., Wen, M., Resnick, L., Goldman, P. & Sherer, J. (2014b).Social Factors that Contribute to Attrition in MOOCs, in *Proceedings of the First ACM Conference on Learning @ Scale.*

Sinha, T., Li, N., Jermann, P., & Dillenbourg, P. (2014). Capturing 'attrition intensifying' structural traits from didactic interaction sequences of MOOC learners, in *Proceedings of the 2014 Empirical Methods in Natural Language Processing Workshop on Modeling Large Scale Social Interaction in Massively Open Online Courses, Qatar, October 2014.*

Sharkey, M. & Sanders, R. (2014). A Process for Predicting MOOC Attrition, in *Proceedings of the 2014 Empirical Methods in Natural Language Processing Workshop on Modeling Large Scale Social Interaction in Massively Open Online Courses, Qatar, October 2014.*

Suthers, D., Lund, K., Rosé, C. P., Teplovs, C., Law, N. (2013). *Productive Multivocality in the Analysis of Group Interactions,* edited volume, Springer.

Wen, M., Yang, D., & Rosé, C. P. (2014b). Linguistic Reflections of Student Engagement in Massive Open Online Courses, in *Proceedings of the International Conference on Weblogs and Social Media*

Wen, M., Yang, D., & Rosé, C. P. (2014a). Sentiment Analysis in MOOC Discussion Forums: What does it tell us? in *Proceedings of Educational Data Mining.*

Yang, D., Sinha, T., Adamson, D., & Rosé, C. P. (2013). Turn on, Tune in, Drop out: Anticipating student dropouts in Massive Open Online Courses, in *NIPS Data-Driven Education Workshop*.

Yang, D., Wen, M., & Rosé, C. P. (2014). Peer Influence on Attrition in Massively Open Online Courses, in *Proceedings of Educational Data Mining.*

Capturing “attrition intensifying” structural traits from didactic interaction sequences of MOOC learners

Tanmay Sinha[1], Nan Li[2], Patrick Jermann[3], Pierre Dillenbourg[2]
[1]Language Technologies Institute, Carnegie Mellon University, Pittsburgh PA 15213, USA
[2]Computer-Human Interaction in Learning and Instruction, EPFL, CH 1015, Switzerland
[3]Center for Digital Education, EPFL, CH 1015, Switzerland
[1]`tanmays@andrew.cmu.edu`, [2,3]`<firstname.lastname>@epfl.ch`

Abstract

This work is an attempt to discover hidden structural configurations in learning activity sequences of students in Massive Open Online Courses (MOOCs). Leveraging combined representations of video clickstream interactions and forum activities, we seek to fundamentally understand traits that are predictive of decreasing engagement over time. Grounded in the interdisciplinary field of network science, we follow a graph based approach to successfully extract indicators of active and passive MOOC participation that reflect persistence and regularity in the overall interaction footprint. Using these rich educational semantics, we focus on the problem of predicting student attrition, one of the major highlights of MOOC literature in the recent years. Our results indicate an improvement over a baseline ngram based approach in capturing “attrition intensifying” features from the learning activities that MOOC learners engage in. Implications for some compelling future research are discussed.

1 Introduction

Massive Open Online Courses (MOOCs) have attracted millions of students, and yet, their pedagogy is often less elaborated than the state of the art in learning sciences. Scaling up learning activities in MOOCs can be viewed as a sacrifice of pedagogical support, made acceptable by the benefits of giving broad access to education for a marginal increase of costs. Even with students volunteering as teaching assistants in MOOCs, it is not possible to provide at a distance the same support quality in a class of ten thousand as in a class of a hundred, because of the difficulty to collect and analyse data from such a high number of learners. This means that MOOC instructors need to rely on rich computational methods that capture the formalism of how learners progress through the course and what traits of decreasing engagement with the course are predictive of attrition over time. The interpretation of the state of the students can then either be performed by the students themselves, by a human coach or by an automated agent that can deliver recommendations to the students.

In this work, we model the sequence of learning activities in the MOOC as a graph with specific properties. Describing the participants actions sequence as a graph may initially sound as a futile complexity since most MOOCs are built as a simple linear sequence of activities (watch video, do assignments, read forums). However, when looking at the activity in more detail, some sequences are richer and justify a more powerful descriptive modeling. The descriptive power of the graph model is to capture the underlying structure of the learning activity. The hypothesis is that formalizing the workflow of such heterogeneous behavior in MOOCs, is one solution to be able to a) scale up learning activities that may initially appear as non scalable, b) help instructors reason out how educational scenarios concretely unfold with time, such as what happened during the course (at what times were learners active and performing well, lost, disoriented or trapped) and what needs to be repaired.

2 Related Work

In this section we outline perspectives on student attrition that have been explored so far in the literature on MOOCs. Much of this work successfully leverages effective feature engineering and advanced statistical methods. However, the biggest limitation of most of these emerging works is that they focus solely on discussion forum behavior or video lecture activity, but do not fuse and take them into account. Some of these works

Proceedings of the 2014 Conference on Empirical Methods in Natural Language Processing (EMNLP), pages 42–49,
October 25-29, 2014, Doha, Qatar.

have grown out of research on predicting academic progress of students and identifying students those who are at dropout risk (Kotsiantis et al., 2003; Dekker et al., 2009; Pal, 2012; Márquez-Vera et al., 2013; Manhaes et al., 2014).

Some prior research has focused on deriving social positioning metrics within discussion forums to understand influencing factors that lead to differently motivated behaviors of students. For example, (Yang et al., 2013; Rosé et al., 2014) used aggregate post-reply discussion forum graph per week, with an aim to investigate posting behavior and collaborative aspects of participation through operationalizations of social positioning. However, we work at a much finer granularity in the current study and our focus is on individual student modeling instead. We capture not only forum participation trajectory, but also video lecture viewing activity of every student in their participation week. Modeling the combined interaction footprint as an activity network, allows us to decipher the type of engagement and organization of behavior for each student, which are reflective of attrition.

Similarly (Ramesh et al., 2014; Wen et al., 2014a; Wen et al., 2014b) published results that describe longitudinal discussion forum behavior affecting student dropout, in terms of posting, viewing, voting activity, level of subjectivity (cognitive engagement) and positivity (sentiment) in students' posts. Related to this, one recent work of (Rossi and Gnawali, 2014) have made an attempt to overcome the language dependency drawback of these works and capture language independent discussion forum features related to structure, popularity, temporal dynamics of threads and diversity of students.

It is important to note, however, that all this substantial research caters to only about 5% of students who participate in MOOC discussion forums (Huang et al., 2014). Our recent work has laid a preliminary foundation for research investigating students' information processing behavior while interacting with MOOC video lectures (Sinha et al., 2014). We apply a cognitive video watching model to explain the dynamic process of cognition involved in MOOC video clickstream interaction and develop a simple, yet potent information processing index that can be effectively used as an operationalization for making predictions regarding critical learner behavior, specifically in-video and course dropouts. In an attempt to better understand what features are predictive of students ceasing to actively participate in the MOOC, (Veeramachaneni et al., 2014) have integrated a crowd sourcing approach for effective feature engineering at scale. Among posting, assignment and grading metrics, students' cohort membership depending on their MOOC engagement was identified as an influential feature for dropout prediction.

3 Study Context

The current study is a part of the shared task for EMNLP 2014 Workshop on Modeling Large Scale Social Interaction in Massively Open Online Courses (Rosé and Siemens, 2014). We have both video clickstream data (JSON) and discussion forum activity data (SQL) from one Coursera MOOC as training data, that we use in this work. Our predictive models will also be tested on 5 other Coursera MOOCs.

In general, Coursera forums, divided into various subforums, have a thread starter post that serves as a prompt for discussion. The thread builds up as people start following up discussions by their posts and comments. As far as our forum dataset is concerned, we have 31532 instances of forum viewing and 35306 instances of thread viewing. In addition to this view data, we have 4840 posts and 2652 comments among 1393 threads initiated in the discussion forums during the span of the course, which received 5060 upvotes and 1763 downvotes in total.

To supplement the forum data, we additionally leverage rich video interaction data from the clickstream data. The clickstream data contains many errors. We obtained 82 unique video ids from the clickstream data, but only 45 of them are valid (watched by large number of unique students). The 37 invalid video ids may be simply due to logging errors. They are also likely to be videos that were uploaded by the course staff for testing purposes. There are in total 27739 students registered the course, however, only 14312 students had online video interactions. The rest of the students may have never logged in, or only have viewed the course pages, or have downloaded the videos without further online engagement. Among the 14312 students who have video interactions, 14264 of them have valid video events logged, which lead to 181100 valid video sessions for our analysis. These valid video sessions further contain

462341 play events, 295103 pause events, 87585 forward jumps, 98169 backward jumps, 6707 forward scrolls, 5311 backward scrolls, 18051 video-play rate increase and 16163 decrease events, respectively.

Our dropout prediction approach that will be described in the next section is applied to student interactions comprising of only online forum and video viewing activities. Currently, we do not make use of the pageview click data.

4 Technical Approach

1. To capture the behaviors exhibited in two primary MOOC activities, namely video lecture viewing and forum interaction, we operationalize the following metrics:
   - **Video lecture clickstream activities**: Play (PL), Pause (PA), SeekFw (FW), SeekBw (BW), ScrollFw (FS), ScrollBw (BS), Ratechange Increase (RCI), Ratechange Decrease (RCD). When two seek events happen in < 1 second, we group them into a scroll. We encode ratechange event based on whether students sped up or slowed down with respect to playrate of the last click event.
   - **Discussion forum activities**: Post (Po), Comment (Co), Thread (Th), Upvote (Uv), Downvote (Dv), Viewforum (Vf), Viewthread (Vt)
2. Because timing of all such MOOC events are logged in our data, we sort all these activities by timestamp to obtain the sequence of activities done by students. This gives us a simple sequentially ordered time series that can be used to reason about behavioral pattern of students.
3. We form the interaction footprint sequence for students by concatenating all their different timestamped MOOC activities for every week of MOOC activity. For example, if a student watched a video (PL, PA, FW, RCI, PA) at [time *'i'*, week *'j'*], viewed a forum at time [*'i+1'*, week *'j'*] and consequently made a post at [time *'i+2'*, week *'j'*], his interaction footprint sequence for week 'j' would be: PL PA FW RCI PA Vf Po. Forming such a sequence captures in some essence, the cognitive mind state that govern students' interaction, as they progress through the MOOC by engaging with these multiple forms of computer mediated inputs. Most MOOCs are based on a weekly rhythm with a new set of videos and new assignments released every week.
4. To find subsequences that might help us to predict student dropout before it occurs, we extract the following set of features for each student in each of his participation weeks:
   - **N-grams** from the interaction footprint sequence (n = 2 to 5). Such 'n' consecutively occurring MOOC activities not only characterize suspicious behaviors that might lead to student attrition but also help us to automatically determine the elements of what might be considered "best MOOC interaction practices" that keep students engaged.
   - **Proportion** of video viewing activities among all video interactions, that are active or passive. We define passive video viewing as mere play and pause (PL, PA), while rest of the video lecture clickstream activities (FW, BW, FS, BS, RCD, RCI) are considered elements of active video viewing.
   - **Proportion** of discussion forum activities among all forum interactions, that are active or passive. We define passive forum activities as viewing a forum or thread (Vf, Vt), upvoting and downvoting (Uv, Dv). The forum activities of starting a thread (Th), posting (Po) and commenting (Co) are indicative of active forum interaction.

In general, because passive video lecture viewing is high (for example, 48% of all video clickstream activities in our dataset comprise of activity sequences having only PL event), discussion forum conversation networks in MOOCs are sparse (only 10% of forum activities relate to explicitly posting, commenting or starting a thread) and passive forum activities are very predominant (90% of forum interactions in our dataset are just passively viewing a thread/forum, upvoting or downvoting), differentiating between such active and passive forms of involvement might clarify participation profiles that are most likely to lead to disengagement of students from the MOOC.

5. In an attempt to enrich the basic ngram representation and better infer traits of active and passive participation, we extract the following set of graph metrics from the overall interaction footprint sequence. Specifically, in this modeling scheme, we extract consecutive windows of length two and create a directed edge of weight one between the activities appearing in sequential order. This results in a directed graph (having self loops and parallel edges), with nodes representing activities done by a student in particular week, while the weighted edges representing the frequencies of activities appearing after one another. For example, in a sequence, (Vt Po Vt Po Po), corresponding nodes in the graph are Vt and Po, while edges are (Vt, Po), (Po, Vt), (Vt, Po) and (Po, Po). The activity graph thus describes the visible part of the educational activities (who does what and when) and models the structure of activity sequences, rather than the details of each activity. Features from the syntactic structure of the graph along with their educational semantics are described below.

    - **Number of nodes and edges**: Indicative of whether overall participation of students in different MOOC activities is high or low.
    - **Density**: Graph density is a tight-knittedness indicator of how involved students are in different MOOC activities, how clustered their activities are or how frequently they switch back and forth between different activities. Technically, for a directed network, density = $m/n(n-1)$, where m=number of edges, n=number of nodes. For our multidigraph representation, density can be >1, because self loops are counted in the total number of edges. This also implies that values of density >1 denote high persistence in doing particular set of MOOC activities, because of greater number of self loops.
    - **Number of self loops**: Though graph density provides meaningful interpretations when > 1, we can't conclusively infer activity persistence in an activity graph with low density. So, we additionally extract number of self loops to refer to the regularity in interaction behavior.
    - **Number of Strongly Connected Components (SCC)**: SCC define a special relationship among a set of graph vertices that can be exploited (each vertex can be reached from every other vertex in the component via a directed path). If the number of SCC in an activity graph are high, there is a high probability that students performs certain set of activities frequently to successfully achieve their desired learning outcomes in the course. This might be an influential indicator for behavioral organization and continuity reflected in overall interaction footprint of students. Dense networks are more likely to have greater number of SCC.
    - **Central activity**: We extract top three activities of students with maximum indegree centrality, for each of their participation weeks. Technically, indegree centrality for a node *'v'* is the fraction of nodes its incoming edges are connected to. Depending on which are the central activities of students, we can characterize how active or passive is the participation. For example, Viewthread and Viewforum (Vt, Vf) are more passive forms of participation than Upvote and Downvote (Uv, Dv), which are in turn more passive than Posting, Commenting, Thread starting (Po, Co, Th) and other intense forms of video lecture participation that represent high grappling with the course material.
    - **Central transition**: We extract the edge (activity transition) with maximum betweenness centrality, which acts like a facilitator in sustaining or decreasing participation. Technically, betweenness centrality of an edge *'e'* is the sum of the fraction of all-pairs shortest paths that pass through *'e'*. We normalize by $1/n(n-1)$ for our directed graphical representation, where *'n'* is the number of nodes. For example, Vt-Po (view thread-post) could be one of the central edges for Th (thread starting activity), which in turn is a strong student

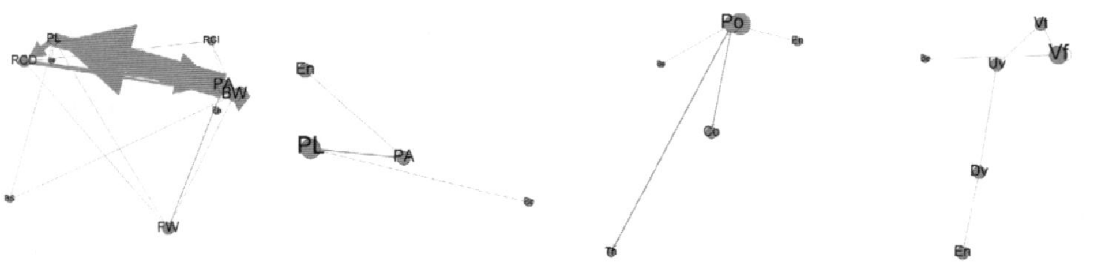

(a) Active video viewing (b) Passive video viewing (c) Active forum activity (d) Passive forum activity

Figure 1: Interaction graphs representing 4 contrasting MOOC scenarios in our dataset

participation indicator. Alternately, Po/Co/Th-Dv (post/comment/thread initiate-downvote) could serve as decision conduits that increase dissatisfaction of students because of others' off content/off-conduct posting. Such lack of exposure to useful and informative posts on forums can potentially aggravate feelings of "lack of peer support" and "healthy community involvement", inturn leading to decreasing engagement.

6. We add certain control variables in our feature set to account for inherently present student characteristics, namely **courseweek** (number of weeks since the course has been running), **userweek** (number of weeks since the student joined the course) and a **nominal variable** indicating whether student activity in a week comprised of only video lecture viewing, only forum activity, both or none.

Because we are interested in investigating a)how behavior within a week affects students' dropout in the next course week, b)how cumulative behavior exhibited up till a week affects students' dropout in the next course week, we create two experimental setups: one using data from the current participation week (***Curr***) and the second using data from the beginning participation week till the current week (***TCurr***). For the second setup, all feature engineering is done from the cumulative interaction footprint sequence.

Some of the interaction graphs culled out from the footprint sequence, which are representative of active and passive MOOC participation are depicted in figure 1. Each graph has a begin (Be) and end (En) node, with nodes sized by indegree centrality and directed edges sized by tie strength.

5 Results

5.1 Evaluating Our Features

As we would intuitively expect, mean and standard deviations for all our extracted graph metrics are higher in the ***TCurr*** setup. Another evident pattern is that all these graph metrics follow long tailed distributions for both ***Curr*** and ***TCurr*** setups, with very few students exhibiting high values. These distributions concur with the 90-9-1 rule in online communities which says that 90% of the participants only view content (for example, watch video, Vf, Vt), 9% of the participants edit content (for example, Uv, Dv), and 1% of the participants actively create new content (for example, Po, Co, Th). Moreover, we notice that the top three central activities with maximum frequency and central edges that describe interactions between them, are passive interaction events. Among the top 20, we can observe central edges such as RCI-RCI or PL-FW that hint towards skipping video and hence decreasing participation, while Th-PL, Po-PL, Th-Po that point towards facilitating participation. Thus, in order to graphically visualize interactions among features and their relationship to the class distribution (dropout and non dropout), we utilize mosaic plot representation. The motivating question being two-fold: a)How do the extracted features vary among dropouts and non dropouts? b)When viewing more than one features together, what can we say about association of different feature combinations to survival of students in the MOOC? After ranking feature projections on basis of interaction gain (in % of class entropy removed), we discern the following:

- For both ***Curr*** and ***TCurr*** setups, the mosaic plots reveal that dropout is higher for students having low number of nodes, edges, SCC and self loops, low activity graph density, low

Model	Performance Metric	Setup *Curr*	Setup *TCurr*
1. Baseline	Accuracy/Kappa	0.623/0.297	0.647/0.173
	False Negative Rate	0.095	0.485
2. Graph	Accuracy/Kappa	0.692/0.365 #	0.693/0.277 #
	False Negative Rate	0.157	0.397
3. Baseline + Graph	Accuracy/Kappa	0.624/0.298	0.646/0.173
	False Negative Rate	0.095	0.482

Table 1: Performance metrics for machine learning experiments. Random classifier performance is 0.5. Values marked # are significantly better (p<0.01, pairwise t-test) than other results in same column

proportion of active forum and video viewing activity. This reflects that our operationalizations drawn from overall interaction footprint are successfully able to capture features expressing student behavior that might escalate attrition.

- Student dropout is higher if they join in later course weeks and have a sparse activity graph. There could be 2 possible explanations: a)Students join later and do minimal activity because they only have specific information needs. So, they do not stay after interacting with the course material in a short non linear fashion and satisfying their needs, b)Students who join later are overwhelmed with lots of introductory and prerequisite MOOC video lectures to watch, pending assignments to be completed to successfully pass the course and discussion forum content already posted. Finding difficulty in coping up with the ongoing pace of the MOOC, they do not stay for prolonged periods in the course.

5.2 Dropout Prediction and Analysis

We leverage machine learning techniques to predict student attrition along the way based on our extracted feature set. The dependent class variable is dropout, which is 0 for all active student participation weeks and 1 only for the last participation week (student ceased to participate in the MOOC after that week), leading to an extremely skewed class distribution. Note that by active student participation, we refer to only forum and video viewing interactions. We construct the following two models for validation. For each model, there is a ***Curr*** and a ***TCurr*** setup:

- **Baseline Ngram Model**: Features used are Coursweek, Userweek, Ngrams from full interaction footprint sequence (2 to 5), Ngram length, proportion of active/passive video viewing and forum activity (dichotomized by equal width), nominal variable.
- **Graph Model**: Features used are Coursweek, Userweek, Ngram length, Graph metrics (top 3 central activities, density (dichotomized by equal frequency), central transition, no. of nodes (dichotomized by equal frequency), no. of edges (dichotomized by equal frequency), no. of self loops (dichotomized by equal frequency), no. of SCC), nominal variable.

For both these models, we use cost sensitive LibSVM with radial basis kernel function (RBF) as the learning algorithm (Hsu et al., 2003). The advantage of RBF is that it nonlinearly maps samples into a higher dimensional space so it, unlike the linear kernel, can handle the case when the relation between class labels and attributes is nonlinear. Rare threshold for feature extraction is set to 4, while cross validation is done using a supplied test set with held out students having sql id 798619 through 1882807.

The important take away messages from these results are:

- Graph model performs significantly better than Baseline ngram model for both ***Curr*** (t=-17.903, p<0.01) and ***TCurr*** (t=-11.834, p<0.01) setups, in terms of higher accuracy/kappa and comparable false negative rates[1]. This is because the graph models the integration of heterogeneous MOOC activities into a structured activity. The edges of the graph, which connect consecutive activities represent a two-fold relationship between these activities: how they relate to each

[1]False negative rate of 0.x means that we correctly identify (100-(100*0.x))% of dropouts

other from a pedagogical and from an operational viewpoint. In addition to capturing just the order and mere presence of active and passive MOOC events scatterred throughout the activity sequence, the activity network representation additionally captures different properties of MOOC interaction such as a)how recurring behaviors develop in the participation trajectory of students, and how the most central ones thrust towards increasing or decreasing engagement, b)how the number and distribution of such activities are indicative of persistence in interaction behavior. The baseline+graph approach does not lead to improvement in results over the baseline approach.

- ***TCurr*** setup does not necessarily lead to better results than ***Curr*** setup. This indicates that students' attrition is more strongly influenced by the most recent week's exhibited behavioral patterns, rather than aggregated MOOC interactions from the beginning of participation. The extremely small false negative rates in ***Curr*** setup indicate the effectiveness of our feature engineering approach in predicting attririon behavior, even with an extremely skewed class distribution. However, more studies would be required to corroborate the relation between change in interaction sequences from one week to another and factors such as students' confusion ("I am unable to follow the course video lectures") or negative exposure ("I am not motivated enough to engage because of less productive discussion forums"), which gradually build up like negative waves before dropout happens (Sinha, 2014).

6 Conclusion and Future Work

In this work, we formed operationalizations that quantify active and passive participation exhibited by students in video lecture viewing and discussion forum behavior. We were successful in developing meaningful indicators of overall interaction footprint that suggest systematization and continuity in behavior, which are in turn predictive of student attrition. In our work going forward, we seek to differentiate the interaction footprint sequences further using potent markov clustering based approaches. The underlying motivation is to decipher sequences having lot of activity overlap as well as similar transition probabilities. These cluster assignments can then serve as features that help segregating interaction sequences predictive of dropout versus non-dropouts.

Another interesting enhancement to our work would include grouping commonly occurring activities that learners perform in conjunction with each other and form higher level latent categories indicative of different participation traits. In our computational work, we have recently been developing techniques for operationalizing video lecture clickstreams of students into cognitively plausible higher level behaviors to aid instructors to better understand MOOC hurdles and reason about unsatisfactory learning outcomes (Sinha et al., 2014).

One limitation of the above work is that we are concerned merely with the timestamped order of activities done by a student and not the time gap between activities appearing in the interaction footprint sequence. The effect of an activity on a subsequent activity often fades out with time, i.e. as the lag between two activities increases: learners forget what they learned in a previous activity. For example, the motivation created at the beginning of a lesson by presenting an interesting application example does not last forever, so as to initiate productive forum discussions. Similarly, the situation of a thread being started (Th) and a post being made (Po) within 60 secs of completing video lecture viewing, might imply a different behavior, than if these forum activities occur five days after video lecture viewing. Therefore, we seek to better understand context of the most and least central activities of students in MOOCs, differentiating between subsequences lying within and outside user specified temporal windows. Our goal is to view the interaction footprint sequence formation in a sequential data mining perspective (Mooney and Roddick, 2013) and discover a)most frequently occurring interaction pathways that lead students to such central activities, b)association rules with high statistical confidences that help MOOC instructors to trace why students engage in certain MOOC activities. For example, a rule of the form AB $\Rightarrow$ C, such as "Vf", "Uv" [15s] $\Rightarrow$ "Po" [30s] (confidence = 0.7), is read as if a student navigated and viewed a forum page followed by doing an upvote within 15 seconds, then within the next 30 seconds he would make a post 70% of the time.

References

Dekker, G. W., Pechenizkiy, M., & Vleeshouwers, J. M. (2009). "Predicting Students Drop Out: A Case Study". *International Working Group on Educational Data Mining.*

Huang, J., Dasgupta, A., Ghosh, A., Manning, J., and Sanders, M. 2014. "Superposter behavior in MOOC forums". *ACM Learing at Scale(L@S)*

Hsu, C. W., Chang, C. C., & Lin, C. J. (2003). "A practical guide to support vector classification"

Kotsiantis, S. B., Pierrakeas, C. J., & Pintelas, P. E. (2003, January). "Preventing student dropout in distance learning using machine learning techniques". *In Knowledge-Based Intelligent Information and Engineering Systems* (pp. 267-274). Springer Berlin Heidelberg.

Manhaes, L. M. B., da Cruz, S. M. S., & Zimbrao, G. (2014, March). "WAVE: an architecture for predicting dropout in undergraduate courses using EDM". *In Proceedings of the 29th Annual ACM Symposium on Applied Computing* (pp. 243-247). ACM.

Márquez-Vera, C., Cano, A., Romero, C., & Ventura, S. (2013). "Predicting student failure at school using genetic programming and different data mining approaches with high dimensional and imbalanced data". *Applied intelligence*, 38(3), 315-330.

Mooney, C. H., & Roddick, J. F. (2013). "Sequential pattern mining–approaches and algorithms". *ACM Computing Surveys (CSUR)*, 45(2), 19.

Pal, S. (2012). "Mining educational data to reduce dropout rates of engineering students". *International Journal of Information Engineering and Electronic Business (IJIEEB)*, 4(2), 1.

Ramesh, A., Goldwasser, D., Huang, B., Daume III, H., & Getoor, L. (2014, June). "Learning latent engagement patterns of students in online courses". *In Twenty-Eighth AAAI Conference on Artificial Intelligence.*

Rosé, C. P., Carlson, R., Yang, D., Wen, M., Resnick, L., Goldman, P., & Sherer, J. (2014, March). "Social factors that contribute to attrition in moocs. *In Proceedings of the first ACM conference on Learning@ scale conference* (pp. 197-198). ACM.

Rosé, C. P., Siemens, G. (2014). "Shared Task on Prediction of Dropout Over Time in Massively Open Online Courses", *Proceedings of the 2014 Empirical Methods in Natural Language Processing Workshop on Modeling Large Scale Social Interaction in Massively Open Online Courses*, Qatar, October, 2014.

Rossi, L. A., & Gnawali, O. "Language Independent Analysis and Classification of Discussion Threads in Coursera MOOC Forums".

Sinha, T., Jermann, P., Li, N., Dillenbourg, P. (2014). "Your click decides your fate: Inferring Information Processing and Attrition Behavior from MOOC Video Clickstream Interactions". *Proceedings of the 2014 Empirical Methods in Natural Language Processing Workshop on Modeling Large Scale Social Interaction in Massively Open Online Courses*, Qatar, October, 2014.

Sinha, T. (2014). "Who negatively influences me? Formalizing diffusion dynamics of negative exposure leading to student attrition in MOOCs". *LTI Student Research Symposium, Carnegie Mellon University*

Veeramachaneni, K., O'Reilly, U. M., & Taylor, C. (2014). "Towards Feature Engineering at Scale for Data from Massive Open Online Courses". *arXiv preprint arXiv:1407.5238.*

Wen, M., Yang, D., & Rosé, C. P. (2014a). "Linguistic Reflections of Student Engagement in Massive Open Online Courses". *In Proceedings of the International Conference on Weblogs and Social Media*

Wen, M., Yang, D., & Rosé, C. P. (2014b). "Sentiment Analysis in MOOC Discussion Forums: What does it tell us?". *In Proceedings of Educational Data Mining*

Yang, D., Sinha T., Adamson D., and Rose, C. P. 2013. "Turn on, Tune in, Drop out: Anticipating student dropouts in Massive Open Online Courses" *In NIPS Workshop on Data Driven Education*

A Process for Predicting MOOC Attrition

Mike Sharkey
President
Blue Canary
Chandler, AZ USA
mike@bluecanarydata.com

Robert Sanders
Sr. Software Engineer
Clairvoyant, LLC
Chandler, AZ USA
robert.sanders@clairvoyantsoft.com

Abstract

The goal of this shared task was to predict attrition in a MOOC through use of the data and logs generated by the course. Our approach to the task reinforces the idea that the process of gathering and structuring the data is more important (and more time consuming) than the predictive model itself. The result of the analysis was that a subset of 15 different data features did a sufficiently good job at predicting whether or not a student would exhibit any activity in the following week.

1 Introduction

Blue Canary is a higher education analytics company located in Chandler, Arizona USA. The company has extensive experience in dealing with academic course/enrollment/retention data and is proud to collaborate with other researchers on the EMNLP 2014 shared task. The goal of the task is to use data from one MOOC, create a model to predict course attrition, and then apply that model to five other MOOCs in order to observe the efficacy of the model across courses. The goal of this paper is to document the process that Blue Canary went through in order to generate the model.

2 Understanding the Problem

In order to successfully complete a task such as this, the team needed the right context to the problem. The context for this particular challenge (using MOOC data to predict attrition) was very familiar to the Blue Canary team. First, the team has developed retention-oriented predictive models for a number of institutions in the past. This experience was vital. Second, the team has worked with data at scale. The MOOC course had 20,000 enrolled students with a log file that generated 1.6 million rows of data. The Blue Canary team has experience working with a large online university that had over 300,000 students generating millions of rows of data on a daily basis. Lastly, all of the team members have participated in at least one MOOC, so the processes and interactions associated with such a course are known.

The combination of all of these factors gave the Blue Canary team the necessary context to tackle the attrition problem from the ground up.

3 Approach to the Problem

As with other such data initiatives, the process is a stepwise iterative one. Each step and iteration provides more insight, allowing the team to refine the prediction.

3.1 Step 1: Feature Extraction

Feature extraction is the process of defining the independent variables (or inputs) for the predictive model. This is arguably the most important step in the process of developing a predictive model. It requires a deep understanding of the source data from a technical side as well as a contextual understanding of how the data relate to the front-end user experience.

Blue Canary used two techniques for feature extraction. The first was experience. Having looked at course activity data and developed predictive models for other courses, we knew the kinds of features that would likely have an impact on the prediction. This experience gave us simplistic features like "number of videos watched" and "total minutes spent in class" to more nuanced features like "attempted quiz without referring to other materials".

The second technique was using visualizations to explore data relationships. The team used the Tableau visualization tool to ingest course activity data and map it across users & weeks. Looking at these relationships visually helped to determine if we should include the features in the modeling or not.

Proceedings of the 2014 Conference on Empirical Methods in Natural Language Processing (EMNLP), pages 50–54,
October 25-29, 2014, Doha, Qatar.

3.2 Step 2: Define Outcome/Prediction

Once the list of features have been developed, next step is to define exactly what it is we are predicting. At a high level, it sounds easy – will the student retain in the class? From a data perspective, though, we need to define what it means to retain. Does it mean that the student submitted the assignment for the week? Watched a video? Simply logged in? Zeroing in on a reliable definition of retention is a part of the process.

3.3 Step 3: Run the Predictive Model

With the input and output data in place, the team needs to run a model to derive a prediction. Blue Canary has consistently used machine learning techniques (as opposed to statistical modeling). As Bogard (2011) alludes to in a blog post comparing the two approaches, Blue Canary's technical expertise combined with an unknown underlying relationship make machine learning our preferred method of analysis. For this analysis, Blue Canary implemented a random forest method using the SciKit python toolset (http://scikit-learn.org/).

3.4 Step 4: Observe/Validate/Iterate

The last step in the process is to observe the outcomes of the modeling, validate the results (both quantitatively and qualitatively) and iterate to improve. When looking at the modeling results, we focused on accuracy. More specifically, we focused on the true positive rate (recall) and the true negative rate individually. The combination of these components equal the accuracy of the model, but we thought it was important to look at both since the application of any such solution would involve treatments for both parties.

Value	Definition
True Positive	# predicted to retain / # actually retained
True Negative	# predicted to attrite / # actual attrition
Accuracy	(True positive + True negative) / population

Table 1: Definition of model accuracy values

3.5 Acknowledging Prior Research

It should be noted that Blue Canary has stood on the shoulders of others who have tackled similar problems in the past. Our choice for analytical methods and features has been inspired by earlier predictive projects like Purdue's Course Signals (Arnold and Pistilli, 2012) and research done at American Public University (Boston et. al., 2011). We also referenced contemporary MOOC research that explored the descriptive (Breslow et. al., 2013), predictive (Taylor et. al., 2014), and social (Rosé et. al., 2014) contributors to attrition.

4 Predicting Attrition for PSY-001

The course in question was from a 2013 Georgia Tech/Coursera MOOC called "Introduction to Psychology as a Science". Blue Canary executed seven iterative steps as explained in the previous section. At the end we came up with a model that used 15 features to predict retention and attrition at an 88% accuracy rate.

4.1 Iteration 1: Feature Extraction

The first iteration didn't result in any prediction. The goal was to explore the data and extract an initial set of features for processing. We also created our training, testing, and hold back data using a 70/15/15 split. Table 2 lists the features we initially extracted from the activity data.

- id
- user_id
- username
- week_id
- week_num
- week_start_date
- week_end_date
- session_count
- url_wiki_edit_count
- url_wiki_view_count
- url_quiz_count
- url_lecture_count
- url_forum_count
- is_english
- ip_count
- most_common_browser
- most_common_browser_date
- browser_count
- unique_quizzes_attempted
- total_quiz_attempts
- average_attempts_per_quiz
- videos_accessed_count
- average_video_per_session
- did_peer_review
- actually_attended

Table 2: Initial list of features

These features were very basic. We didn't spend much time on more advanced features. The goal of this first was simply to lay the foundation for our data analysis pipeline.

4.2 Iteration 2: Test Analytical API's

With a bulk of the features in place, our next goal was to connect the machine learning toolset to the pipeline. We used Weka (http://www.cs.waikato.ac.nz/ml/weka/) since the team had some experience with the tool. Since our approach was to construct the pipeline as a smooth-running application, we utilized the Weka API's to feed data in and get results out.

Unfortunately, we ran into technical problems with the API's and got out of memory exception errors. We were unable to troubleshoot and decided to move on to another toolset. In addition, though, we added more features, mainly from parsing the URL strings in the access log files (Table 3).

- event_count
- total_minutes_spent
- url_quiz_submits_count
- url_quiz_actual_submits_count
- url_quiz_percent_of_actual_submits
- url_quiz_attempt_in_more_than_one_session
- url_quiz_retry
- url_quiz_attempt_but_no_submit
- url_quiz_submit_no_help
- url_human_grading_count
- url_forum_search_count
- url_class_preferences_count
- url_signature_count

Table 3: URL features added

4.3 Iteration 3: Too Good to be True

We switched to SciKit as our analytical tool of choice, but we still used the Random Forest method. We ran our first analysis and got the corresponding accuracy rates. As explained in section 3.4, we produce accuracy rates for 'False' (correctly predicting that the student won't attend next week), 'True' (correctly predicting that the student will attend next week) and 'Average' (accuracy – the weighted average of False and True). The results for our first run were as follows:

Measure	Rate
False	99%
True	87%
Accuracy	96%

The team was skeptical about such high accuracy rates, especially given that it was our first run. We suspected that there was some sort of leakage – information about the prediction field may have leaked into one of the features. That suspicion was confirmed when we dug deeper into the model.

The predominant feature was "is_english". We looked at the user agent data in the activity logs and parsed the language parameter to determine if the web browser language was set to English or not. It turns out that when there was no activity for the week, we populated this field with null values. Since the majority of the students had English as their language, the model was seeing "is_english" = TRUE when there was activity and "is_english" = FALSE when there wasn't activity. This was a great example of the kinds of errors one finds early on in the analysis.

4.4 Iteration 4: First Real Model

For the next iteration, we fixed the "is_english" field and ran the model again. This run was our first valid predictive model for the dataset and the results were:

Measure	Rate
False	92%
True	55%
Accuracy	89%

Note that we are doing a very good job at predicting students who won't attend next week. This is due to the fact that there are a large number of students don't attend. We estimated that about 20,000 students signed up for the class, 11,000 of them showed any activity at all, and less than 3,000 completed the course.

4.5 Iteration 5: Defining the Outcome

For experimentation purposes, we wanted to see if changing the definition of "attending" would have any effect on the modeling. Our original definition of attending was that there were ANY user actions in the data (viewing a page, posting a discussion item, taking a quiz, etc.). We decided to add variations to that definition such as "viewing at least one lecture", "submitting at least one quiz", or "will never attend again" (as opposed to just not attending next week). The table below is a sampling of some of the results we generated:

Measure	Out_i	Out_a	Out_b	Out_c
False	92%	94%	97%	87%
True	55%	45%	47%	90%
Accuracy	89%	91%	95%	89%

This exercise showed some interesting results. Specifically, we saw how we would improve our ability to predict students who wouldn't attend (False) but decrease the True accuracy. We did see significant improvement in the case where the outcome was "will never attend again". However, we decided to stay with our base definition of attendance as "no activity in the following week". Validating these alternate definitions of attendance is a task that would be worthwhile for additional research.

4.6 Iteration 6: Team Collaboration

Blue Canary prides itself on collaboration not only amongst researchers in the learning analytics field, but also collaboration inside of our own company. We made sure to share information about this shared task with others in the company, and that collaboration allowed us to positively expand our feature set. One employee had come across MOOC research that had found good predictive results when using an aggregate engagement/activity score (Poellhuber, 2014). We decided to utilize a similar feature where the number of sessions, pages, days, and hours of activity in a given week were combined into an engagement score.

4.7 Iteration 7: Winnowing the Field

As a final step, we wanted to reduce the number of features used in the modeling process so as to improve cycle times. We knew that the majority of the fields had little to no predictive value, so we ran models where we just used the top 10, 15, or 20 features. In the end, all permutations gave similar accuracy scores and we decided to use the top 15 features. Those features resulted in accuracy rates of:

Measure	Rate
False	92%
True	54%
Accuracy	88%

The accuracy rates are similar to the rates we had been getting in the past two iterations of the modeling. This led us to conclude that we were at the point of diminishing returns and we decided to finalize the model with the 15 features and their corresponding importance level as illustrated in Table 4 (below).

Feature	Import.
total_minutes_spent_previous_wk	0.336
initial_activity_score_previous_wk	0.072
final_activity_score_previous_wk	0.071
final_activity_score_up_to_wk	0.070
event_count_up_to_wk	0.068
most_common_browser_count_up_to_wk	0.059
initial_activity_score_up_to_wk	0.049
url_wiki_view_count_up_to_wk	0.041
session_count_up_to_wk	0.038
url_quiz_count_up_to_wk	0.037
total_minutes_spent_up_to_wk	0.037
url_lecture_count_up_to_wk	0.037
browser_count_up_to_wk	0.031
ip_count_up_to_wk	0.031
session_count_previous_wk	0.023

Table 4: Features and Importance

5 Conclusions

The overarching conclusion from this research can be summarized in two points:

1. Machine learning models can do an above average job at predicting retention/attrition in MOOC's
2. The predictive factors are not surprising – they are variants of measures of the student's engagement and activity in the course

5.1 Features

Looking at the features in Table 4, one can see that almost all of the important features are measures of activity. Minutes, events, views and even the aggregated activity feature are all measuring similar characteristics. The takeaway here is that there shouldn't be an expectation of some unique marker that predicts retention. There's no secret in the secret sauce.

6 Acknowledgements

The authors would like to thank Mohammed Ansari, Andy Allen, Satish Divakarla, David Morgan, and the entire Blue Canary and Clairvoyant team for their support in this shared task.

References

Matt Bogard. (2011, January 29) Culture War: Classical Statistics vs. Machine Learning. Retrieved from http://econometricsense.blogspot.com/2011/01/classical-statistics-vs-machine.html

Arnold, K. E., & Pistilli, M. D. (2012, April). Course Signals at Purdue: Using learning analytics to increase student success. In Proceedings of the 2nd International Conference on Learning Analytics and Knowledge (pp. 267-270). ACM.

Boston, W. E., Ice, P., & Gibson, A. M. (2011). Comprehensive assessment of student retention in online learning environments. Online Journal of Distance Learning Administration, 14(4).

Breslow, L., Pritchard, D. E., DeBoer, J., Stump, G. S., Ho, A. D., & Seaton, D. T. (2013). Studying learning in the worldwide classroom: Research into edX's first MOOC. Research & Practice in Assessment, 8, 13-25.

Taylor, C., Veeramachaneni, K., & O'Reilly, U. M. (2014). Likely to stop? Predicting Stopout in Massive Open Online Courses. arXiv preprint arXiv:1408.3382.

Rosé, C. P., Carlson, R., Yang, D., Wen, M., Resnick, L., Goldman, P., & Sherer, J. (2014, March). Social factors that contribute to attrition in moocs. In Proceedings of the first ACM conference on Learning@ scale conference (pp. 197-198). ACM.

Poellhuber, B., Roy, N., Bouchoucha, I., Anderson, T. (2014, April). The Relationship Between the Motivational Profiles, Engagement Profiles and Persistence of MOOC Participants. Retrieved from http://www.moocresearch.com/wp-content/uploads/2014/06/MOOC-Research-InitiativePoelhuber9187v4a.pdf, September 1, 2014.

Predicting Attrition Along the Way: The UIUC Model

Bussaba Amnueypornsakul, Suma Bhat and Phakpoom Chinprutthiwong
University of Illinois,
Urbana-Champaign, USA
{amnueyp1,spbhat2,chinpru2}@illinois.edu

Abstract

Discussion forum and clickstream are two primary data streams that enable mining of student behavior in a massively open online course. A student's participation in the discussion forum gives direct access to the opinions and concerns of the student. However, the low participation (5-10%) in discussion forums, prompts the modeling of user behavior based on clickstream information. Here we study a predictive model for learner attrition on a given week using information mined just from the clickstream. Features that are related to the quiz attempt/submission and those that capture interaction with various course components are found to be reasonable predictors of attrition in a given week.

1 Introduction

As an emerging area that promises new horizons in the landscape resulting from the merger of technology and pedagogy massively open online courses (MOOCs) offer unprecedented avenues for analyzing many aspects of learning at scales not imagine before. The concept though in its incipient stages offers a fertile ground for analyzing learner characteristics that span demographies, learning styles, and motivating factors. At the same time, their asynchronous and impersonal approach to learning and teaching, gives rise to several challenges, one of which is student retention.

In the absence of a personal communication between the teacher and the student in such a scenario, it becomes imperative to be able to understand class dynamics based on the course logs that are available. This serves the efforts of the instructor to better attend to the needs of the class at large. One such analysis is to be able to predict if a student will drop out or continue his/her participation in the course which is the shared task of the EMNLP 2014 Workshop on Modeling Large Scale Social Interaction in Massively Open Online Courses (Rose and Siemens, 2014).

Our approach is to model student attrition as being a function of interaction with various course components.

2 Related Works

The task of predicting student behavior has been the topic of several recent studies. In this context course logs have been analyzed with an effort to predict students? behavior. The available studies can be classified based on the type of course data that has been used for the analysis as those using discussion forum data and those using clickstream data.

Studies using only discussion forum to understand user-behavior rely only on available discussion forum posts as their source of information. In this context, in (Rosé et al., 2014) it was observed that students' forum activity in the first week can reasonably predict the likelihood of users dropping out. Taking a sentiment analysis approach, Wen et al. (Wen et al., 2014b) observed a correlation between user sentiments expressed via forum posts and their chance of dropping out. Motivation being a crucial aspect for a successful online learning experience, (Wen et al., 2014a) employs computational linguistic models to measure learner motivation and cognitive engagement from the text of forum posts and observe that participation in discussion forums is a strong indicator of student commitment.

Even though discussion forum serves as a rich source of information that offers insights into many aspects of student behavior, it has been observed that a very small percentage of students (5-10%) actually participate in the discussion forum. As an alternate data trace of student interaction with the course material, the clickstream

Proceedings of the 2014 Conference on Empirical Methods in Natural Language Processing (EMNLP), pages 55–59,
October 25-29, 2014, Doha, Qatar.

data of users contains a wider range of information affording other perspectives of student behavior. This is the theme of studies such as (Guo and Reinecke, 2014), which is focused on the navigation behavior of various demographic groups, (Kizilcec et al., 2013) which seeks to understand how students engage with the course, (Ramesh et al., 2014), that attempts to understand student disengagement and their learning patterns towards minimizing dropout rate and (Stephens-Martinez et al., 2014) which seeks to model motivations of users by mining clickstream data.

In this study, the task is to predict if a user will stay in the course or drop out using information from forum posts and clickstream information. Our approach is to use only clickstream information and is motivated by key insights such as interaction with the various course components and quiz attempt/submission.

3 Data

Data from one MOOC with approximately 30K students was distributed as training data. This included discussion post information and clickstream information of the students with completely anonymized user ids. Of this a subset of 6583 users was considered the held-out dataset on which we report the performance of the model.

3.1 Preprocessing Stage

Since participants (posters) in the discussion forum constitute a very small minority of the users in a course (between 5-10% as observed in prior studies), we mine the clickstream information for course-interaction. From the clickstream we extract the following information to indicate involvement in the course.

- Total watch time: From the video view information the amount of time watched is calculated by taking the summation of the difference between the time of the last event a user interacts with a video and the initial time a user starts the same video. If a user is idle for longer than 50 minutes, we add the difference between the current time before the user goes idle and the time the user initially interacts with the video to the total time. The new initial time will be after the user goes active again. Then we repeat the process until there is no more viewing action in the clickstream for that user.
- Number of quiz attempts;
- Number of quiz submissions;
- Number of times a user visits the discussion forum;
- Number of times a user posts: The number of times a user posts in a forum is counted. This count includes whether the user starts a thread, posts, or comments.
- Action sequence: We define an *action sequence* of a given user as being the sequence of course-related activity in a given week for a given user. It captures the user's interaction with the various components of a course in chronological order, such as seeking information on the course-wiki, watching a lecture video, posting in the discussion forum. The activities are, p = forum post, a = quiz attempt, s = quiz submit, l = lecture page view, d = lecture download, f = forum view, w = wiki page visited, t = learning tool page visited, o = play video. As an example, the action sequence of a user **wwaaws** in a given week indicates that the user began the course-activity with a visit to the course wiki, followed by another visit to the wiki, then attempted the quiz two successive times and finally submitted the quiz.

Each of the items listed above, captures important aspects of interaction with the course serving as an index of attrition; the more a user interacts with the course in a given week, the less the chances are of dropping out in that week.

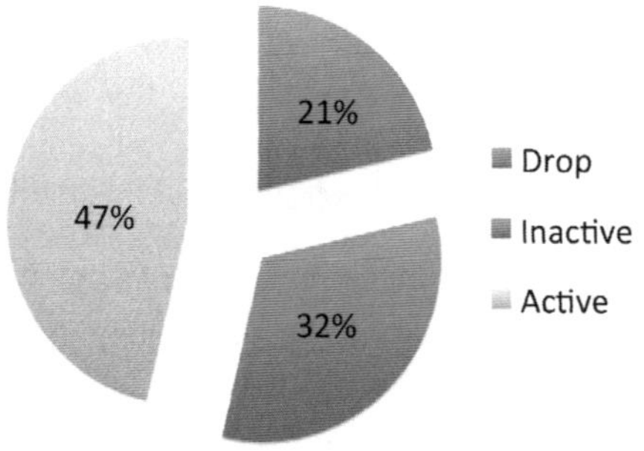

Figure 1: Percentage of each type of users

An exploratory analysis of the data reveals that there are three classes of users based on their interaction with the course components as revealed by the clickstream activity. More specifically, with respect to the length of their action sequence, the 3 classes are:

1. **Active**: This class is the majority class represented by 47% of the users in the course. The users actively interact with more than one component of the course and their enrollment status shows that they did not drop.

2. **Drop**: This is the class represented by a relative minority of the users (21%). The users hardly interact with the course and from their enrollment status they have dropped.

3. **Inactive**: This class of students, represented by 32% of the course, shares commonalities with the first two classes. Whereas their enrollment status indicates that they have not dropped (similar to the **Active** group), their clickstream information shows that their level of course activity is similar to that of the **Drop** class (as evidenced by the length of their action sequence. We define a user to be *inactive* if the action sequence is less than 2 and the user is still enrolled in the course.

The distribution of the three classes of users in the training data is shown in Figure 1. This key observation of the presence of three classes of users prompts us to consider three models to predict user attrition on any given week since we only predict whether a user dropped or not.

1. Mode 1 (Mod1): Inactive users are modeled to be users that dropped because of their similar activity pattern;

2. Mode 2 (Mod2): Inactive users are modeled as **Active** users because they did not formally drop out;

3. Mode 3 (Mod3): Inactive users are modeled as **Drop** with a probability of 0.5 and **Active** with a probability of 0.5. This is because they share status attributes with **Active** and interaction attributes with **Drop**.

4 Features

We use two classes of features to represent user-behavior in a course and summarize them as follows.

- Quiz related: The features in this class are: whether a user submitted the quiz (binary), whether a user attempted the quiz (binary), whether a user attempted but did not submit the quiz (binary). The intuition behind this set of features is that in general quiz-related activity denotes a more committed student with a higher level of involvement with the course. This set is also intended to capture three levels of commitment, ranging from only an attempt at the lowest level, attempting but not submitting at a medium level, to submitting the quiz being the highest level.

- Activity related: The features in this category are derived from the action sequence of the user during that week and they are:

  1. Length of the action sequence (numeric);
  2. The number of times each activity (p, a, s, l, d, f, w, o, or t) occurred (numeric);
  3. The number of wiki page visits/length of the action sequence (numeric).

  The features essentially capture the degree of involvement as a whole and the extent of interaction with each component.

5 Experiments

5.1 Models

We consider two input data distributions of the training data: a) a **specific** case, where the inactive users are excluded. In this case, the model is trained only on users that are either active or those that have dropped. b) a **general** case, where the inactive users are included as is. In both cases, the testing data has the inactive users included, but are either modeled as Mode 1, 2 or 3. This results in 6 models {specific, general} x {Mode1, Mode2, Mode3}.

We train an SVM for each model and observe that an *rbf* kernel achieves the best accuracy among the kernel choices. We use the scikit implementation of SVM (Pedregosa et al., 2011). The parameter γ was tuned to maximize accuracy via 5 fold cross validation on the entire training set. We observe that the performance of Mode 3 was much lower than that of Modes 1 and 2 and thus exclude it from the results.

The tuned models were finally evaluated for accuracy, precision, recall, F-measure and Cohen's

κ on the held-out dataset.

5.2 Experimental Results

	Mode 1		**Mode 2**	
	Specific	General	Specific	General
Baseline	46.42%	46.42%	78.66%	78.66%
Accuracy	**91.31%**	85.34%	78.48%	**78.56%**

Table 1: Accuracy of the models after parameter tuning.

We compare the accuracy of the tuned models with a simple baseline which classifies a user, who, during a given week, submits the quiz and has an action sequence length more than 1 as one who will not drop. The baseline accuracy is 46.42% for Mode 1 and 78.66% for Mode 2. We observe that modeling the inactive user as one who drops performs significantly better than the baseline, whereas modeling the inactive user as one who stays, does not improve the baseline. This is summarized in Table 1.

Of these models we chose two of the best performing models and evaluate them on the held-out data. The chosen models were: Model 1 = (specific,Mode1) and Model 2 = (general,Mode2). The resulting tuned Model 1 (inactive = drop) had $\gamma = 0.1$ and Model 2 (inactive = stay) had a $\gamma = 0.3$ and C as the default value.

	Model 1	**Model 2**
Accuracy	50.98%	80.40%
Cohen's Kappa	-0.06	0.065
P	0.167	0.482
R	0.371	0.058
F	0.228	0.104

Table 2: Accuracy, Cohen's kappa, Precision (P), Recall (R) and F-measure (F) scores for the models on the held-out data.

The performance (accuracy, Cohen's κ, precision, recall and F-measure scores of the two models on the held-out data are shown in Table 2. The final model submitted for evaluation on the test set is Model 2. It was more general since its training data included the inactive users as well. However, the skew in the data distribution is even larger for this model.

We highlight some important observations based on the result.

- Model 2, which is trained to be more general and has the inactive users included, but operates in Mode 2 (regards inactive users as active) has a better accuracy compared to Model 1, which is trained by excluding the inactive users, but operates in Mode 1 (regards inactive users as drop).
- In terms of the κ score, Model 2 shows some agreement, but Model 1 shows no agreement.
- The increased accuracy of Model 2 comes at the expense of reduced recall. This suggests that Model 2 has more false negatives compared to Model 1 on the held-out set.
- Even with reduced recall, Model 2 is more precise than Model 1. This implies that Model 1 tends to infer a larger fraction of false positives compared to Model 2.

6 Discussion

6.1 Data Imbalance

The impact of class imbalance on the SVM classifier is well-known to result in the majority class being well represented compared to the minority class (Longadge and Dongre, 2013). In our modeling with different input data distributions as in the *specific* case (Model 1), where we exclude inactive users, the data imbalance could have significantly affected the performance. This is because, the class of active users is more than double the size of the class of users who dropped.

Our attempt to counter the effect of the minority class by oversampling, resulted in no improvement in performance. In future explorations, other efforts to counter the data imbalance may be helpful.

6.2 Parameter tuning

The models studied here were tuned to maximize accuracy. In the future, models that are tuned to maximize Cohen's κ may be worth exploring.

6.3 Ablation Analysis

	Quiz Related	Activity Related
Model 1	80.48%	50.95%
Model 2	80.48%	80.41%

Table 3: Accuracy and kappa scores for the models by removing the corresponding set of features.

Table 3 summarizes the results of the ablation study conducted for each model by removing each class of features. For **Model 1**, the activity-related features constitute the most important set of features as seen by the drop in accuracy resulting from its omission. For **Model 2**, however, both sets of features have nearly the same effect.

References

Philip J. Guo and Katharina Reinecke. 2014. Demographic differences in how students navigate through moocs. In *Proceedings of the First ACM Conference on Learning @ Scale Conference*, L@S '14, pages 21–30, New York, NY, USA. ACM.

René F. Kizilcec, Chris Piech, and Emily Schneider. 2013. Deconstructing disengagement: Analyzing learner subpopulations in massive open online courses. In *Proceedings of the Third International Conference on Learning Analytics and Knowledge*, LAK '13, pages 170–179, New York, NY, USA. ACM.

R. Longadge and S. Dongre. 2013. Class Imbalance Problem in Data Mining Review. *ArXiv e-prints*, May.

F. Pedregosa, G. Varoquaux, A. Gramfort, V. Michel, B. Thirion, O. Grisel, M. Blondel, P. Prettenhofer, R. Weiss, V. Dubourg, J. Vanderplas, A. Passos, D. Cournapeau, M. Brucher, M. Perrot, and E. Duchesnay. 2011. Scikit-learn: Machine learning in Python. *Journal of Machine Learning Research*, 12:2825–2830.

Arti Ramesh, Dan Goldwasser, Bert Huang, Hal Daume III, and Lise Getoor. 2014. Uncovering hidden engagement patterns for predicting learner performance in moocs. In *ACM Conference on Learning at Scale*, Annual Conference Series. ACM, ACM Press.

Carolyn Rose and George Siemens. 2014. Shared task on prediction of dropout over time in massively open online courses. In *Proceedings of the 2014 Empirical Methods in Natural Language Processing Workshop on Modeling Large Scale Social Interaction in Massively Open Online Courses.*

Carolyn Penstein Rosé, Ryan Carlson, Diyi Yang, Miaomiao Wen, Lauren Resnick, Pam Goldman, and Jennifer Sherer. 2014. Social factors that contribute to attrition in moocs. In *Proceedings of the First ACM Conference on Learning @ Scale Conference*, L@S '14, pages 197–198, New York, NY, USA. ACM.

Kristin Stephens-Martinez, Marti A. Hearst, and Armando Fox. 2014. Monitoring moocs: Which information sources do instructors value? In *Proceedings of the First ACM Conference on Learning @ Scale Conference*, L@S '14, pages 79–88, New York, NY, USA. ACM.

Miaomiao Wen, Diyi Yang, and Carolyn Penstein Rosé. 2014a. Linguistic reflections of student engagement in massive open online courses. In *ICWSM*.

Miaomiao Wen, Diyi Yang, and Carolyn Penstein Rosé. 2014b. Sentiment analysis in mooc discussion forums: What does it tell us? In *the 7th International Conference on Educational Data Mining*.

Predicting MOOC Dropout over Weeks Using Machine Learning Methods

Marius Kloft, Felix Stiehler, Zhilin Zheng, Niels Pinkwart
Department of Computer Science
Humboldt University of Berlin
Berlin, Germany
{kloft, felix.stiehler, zhilin.zheng, pinkwart}@hu-berlin.de

Abstract

With high dropout rates as observed in many current larger-scale online courses, mechanisms that are able to predict student dropout become increasingly important. While this problem is partially solved for students that are active in online forums, this is not yet the case for the more general student population. In this paper, we present an approach that works on click-stream data. Among other features, the machine learning algorithm takes the weekly history of student data into account and thus is able to notice changes in student behavior over time. In the later phases of a course (i.e., once such history data is available), this approach is able to predict dropout significantly better than baseline methods.

1 Introduction

In the past few years, with their dramatically increasing popularity, Massive Open Online Courses (MOOCs) have become a way of online learning used across the world by millions of people. As a result of efforts conducted (sometimes jointly) by academia and industry, many MOOC providers (such as Coursera, Udacity, Edx, or iversity) have emerged, which are able to deliver well-designed online courses to learners. In typical MOOC platforms, learners can not only access lecture videos, assignments and examinations, but can also use collaborative learning features such as online discussion forums. Despite all the MOOC features and benefits, however, one of the critical issues related to MOOCs is their high dropout rate, which puts the efficacy of the learning technology into question. According to the online data provided by Jordan (2014), most MOOCs have completion rates of less than 13%. While discussions are still ongoing as to whether these numbers are actually a problem indicating partial MOOC failures or whether they merely indicate that the community of MOOC learners is diverse and by far not every participant intends to complete a course, researchers and MOOC providers are certainly interested in methods for increasing completion rates. The analysis of MOOC data can be of help here. For instance, a linguistic analysis of the MOOC forum data can discover valuable indicators for predicting dropout of students (Wen et al., 2014). However, only few MOOC students (roughly 5-10%) use the discussion forums (Rose and Siemens, 2014), so that dropout predictors for the remaining 90% would be desirable. In order to get insights into the learning behaviors of this majority of participants, the clickstream data of the MOOC platform usage is the primary source for analysis in addition to the forum data. That is also the motivation of the shared task proposed by the MOOC workshop at the Conference on Empirical Methods in Natural Language Processing (EMNLP 2014) (Rose and Siemens, 2014). Addressing this task, we propose a machine learning method based on support vector machines for predicting dropout between MOOC course weeks in this paper.

The rest of this paper is organized as follows. We begin with the description of the data set and features extracted from the data set. We then describe our prediction model. Next, the prediction results and some experimental findings are presented. Finally, we conclude our work in this paper.

2 Dataset

The dataset we used in this paper was prepared for the shared task launched by the Modeling Large Scale Social Interaction in Massively Open Online Courses Workshop at the Conference on Empirical Methods in Natural Language Processing

Proceedings of the 2014 Conference on Empirical Methods in Natural Language Processing (EMNLP), pages 60–65,
October 25-29, 2014, Doha, Qatar.

(EMNLP 2014) (Rose and Siemens, 2014). The data was collected from a psychology MOOC course which was launched in March 2013. The whole course lasted for 12 weeks with 11,607 participants in the beginning week and 3,861 participants staying until the last course week. Overall, 20,828 students participated, with approximately 81.4% lost at last. Note that the data cover the whole life cycle of this online course up to 19 weeks. The original dataset for this task had two types of data: clickstream data and forum data. In this paper, we only make use of clickstream data to train our prediction model and we do not further consider forum data. Obviously, this will lower the prediction quality for the 5% of students that use the forum, but it will hopefully shed light on the utility of the clickstream data for the larger set of all participants. The clickstream data includes 3,475,485 web log records which can be generally classified into two types: the page view log and the lecture video log. In the following section, we will describe attributes extracted from the raw clickstream data which (we believed) could be correlated to drop-out over the 12 course weeks.

2.1 Attributes description

Our model is an attempt to predict the participants' drop-out during the next week (defined as no activity in that week and in any future week) using the data of the current and past weeks. Consequently, all attributes are computed for each participant and for each week. Note that this results in having more data for later course weeks, since the approach allows for comparing a student's current activity with the activity of that student in the past weeks. The complete attributes list is shown in Table 1.

2.2 Attribute Generation

The attributes required for the predictions are extracted by parsing the clickstream file where each line represents a web request. For each line the corresponding Coursera ID is taken from the database containing the forum data and the course week is calculated from the timestamp relative to the start date of the course. Then the request is analysed regarding its type and every present attribute is saved.

After collecting the raw attributes, the data needs to be post-processed. There are 3 kinds of attributes: attributes that need to be summed up, attributes that need to be averaged and attributes that need to be decided by majority vote. After the post-processing the data consists of lists of attributes each correlated to a unique tuple consisting of the Coursera ID and the course week number. Invalid attributes are getting replaced with the median of that week. Note that every missing week is getting replaced by the median of the attributes of active users in that week that were also active in the original week.

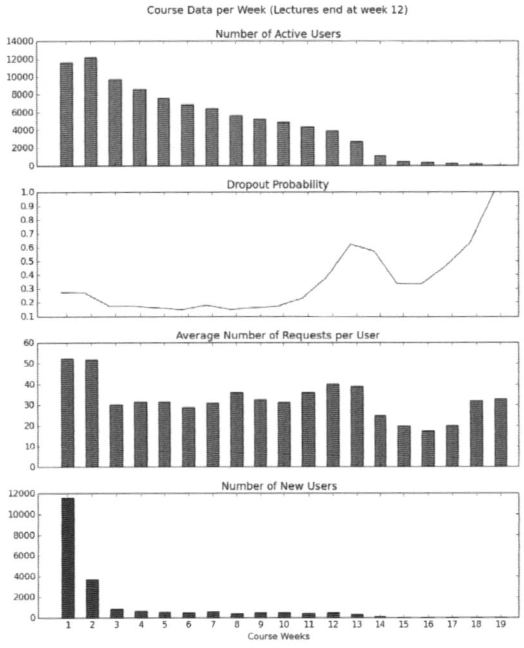

Figure 1: Several basic properties of the analyzed data set.

2.3 A First Glance on the Data Set

We have visualized several basic properties of the data in Figure 1. We observe that the number of active user quickly decreases over time. Furthermore the dropout probability is especially high in the first two weeks, and then of course at the end of the course starting around week 11 and 12.

3 Methodology & Results

In this section we concisely describe the employed feature extraction and selection pipeline, as well as the employed machine learning algorithms. For each week of the course ($i = 1, \ldots, 19$) we computed the dropout label of each of the n_i participants (user ids) being active in that week, based on checking whether there is any activity associated to the same user id in proceeding next week.

ID	Attributes
1	**Number of requests**: total number of requests including page views and video click actions
2	**Number of sessions:** number of sessions is supposed to be a reflection of high engagement, because more sessions indicate more often logging into the learning platform
3	**Number of active days:** we define a day as an active day if the student had at least one session on that day
4	**Number of page views:** the page views include lecture pages, wiki pages, homework pages and forum pages
5	**Number of page views per session:** the average number of pages viewed by each participant per session
6	**Number of video views:** total number of video click actions
7	**Number of video views per session:** average number of video click actions per session
8	**Number of forum views:** number of course discussion forum views
9	**Number of wiki views:** number of course wiki page views
10	**Number of homework page views**
11	**Number of straight-through video plays:** this is a video action attribute. Straight-trough playing video means that the participates played video without any jump (e.g. pause, resume, jump backward and jump forward). Since the lecture videos are the most important learning resource for the learning participants, the video playing should be investigated as other researchers did (Brotherton and Abowd, 2004). In this paper, five video behaviors are taken into account including the number of full plays as well as four others: start-stop during video plays, skip-ahead during video plays, relisten during video plays and the use of low play rate
12	**Number of start-stop during video plays:** start-stop during video plays stands for a lecture video being paused and resumed
13	**Number of skip-ahead during video plays:** skip-ahead means that the participant played a video with a forward jump
14	**Number of relisten during video plays:** relisten means that a backward jump was made as the participant was playing a video
15	**Number of slow play rate use:** this attribute is considered as an indicator of weak understanding of the lecturer's lecture presentation, possibly because of language difficulties or a lack of relevant background knowledge
16	**Most common request time:** our attempt with this attribute is to separate day time learning from night time learning. We define night time from 19:00 to 6:59 in the morning and the other half day as day time
17	**Number of requests from outside of Coursera:** this is to discover how many requests from third-party tools (such as e-mail clients and social networks) to the course were made, which could be an indicator of the participant's social behavior
18	**Number of screen pixels:** the screen pixels is an indicator of the device that the student used. Typically, mobile devices come with fewer pixels
19	**Most active day:** through this attribute, we can investigate if starting late or early could have an impact on dropout
20	**Country:** this information could reflect geographical differences in learning across the world
21	**Operating System**
22	**Browser**

Table 1: Attributes list.

This resulted in label vectors $y_i \in \{-1, 1\}^{n_i}$ for $i = 1, \ldots, 19$, where $+1$ indicates dropout (and thus -1 indicates no dropout). We experimented on the 22 numerical features described in the previous section. The features with ids 1–19 could be represented a single real number, while all other features had to be embedded into a multidimensional space. For simplicity we thus first focused on features 1–19. For each week i of the course, this results in a matrix $X_i^{\text{preliminary}} \in \mathbb{R}^{19 \times n_i}$, the rows and columns of which correspond to the features and user ids, respectively. We then enriched the matrices by considering also the "history" of the features, that is, for the data of week i, all the features of the previous weeks were appended (as additional rows) to the actual data matrix, resulting in $X_i \in \mathbb{R}^{19i \times n_i}$. We can write this as $X_i = (x_1, \ldots, x_{n_i})$, where x_j is the feature vector of the jth user. Box plots of these features showed that the distribution is highly skewed and non-normal, and furthermore all features are non-negative. We thus tried two standard features transformations: 1. logarithmic transformation 2. box-cox transformation. Subsequent box plots indicated that both lead to fairly non-skewed distributions. The logarithmic transformation is however much faster and lead to better results in later pipeline steps, which is why it was taken for the remaining experiments.

Subsequently, all features were centered and normalized to unit standard deviation. We then performed simple t-tests for each feature and computed also the Fisher score $f_j = \sqrt{\frac{\mu_+ - \mu_-}{\sigma_+^2 + \sigma_-^2}}$, where $\mu_\pm$ and $\sigma_\pm^2$ are the mean and variance of the positive (dropout) and negative class, respectively. Both t-tests and Fisher scores lead to comparable results; however, we have made superior experiences with the Fisher score, which is why we focus on this approach in the following methodology. We found that the video features (id 11–15), the most common request time (id 17), and the most active day feature (id 19) consistently achieved scores very close to zero, which is why they were discarded. The remaining features are shown in Figure 2 (a similar plot was generated using t-tests and found to be consistent with the Fisher scores, but is omitted due to space constraints). The results indicate that features related to a more balanced behaviour pattern over the course of a week (especially the number of sessions and number of active days) were (weakly) predictive of dropout in the beginning of the course. From week 6 to 12 we could also measure a rising importance of the number of wiki page views (id 9) and homework submission page views (id 10). Past week 12 features related to activity in a more general way like the number of requests (id 1) or the number of page views (id 4) became the most predicative.

We proceeded with an exploratory analysis, where we performed a principal component analysis (PCA) for each week, the result is shown in Figure 3. The plot indicates that the users that have dropped out can be better separated from the users that did not drop out when the week id increases. To follow up on this we trained, for each week, a linear support vector machine (SVM) (Cortes and Vapnik, 1995) using the `-s 2` option in LIBLINEAR (Fan et al., 2008), which is one of the fastest solvers to train linear SVMs (Fan et al., 2008). The SVM computes an affine-linear prediction function $f(x) := \langle w, x \rangle + b$, based on maximizing the (soft) margin between positive and negative examples: $(w, b) := \text{argmin}_{w,b} \frac{1}{2}||w||^2 + C \sum_{i=1}^{n} \max(0, 1 - y_i(\langle w, x_i \rangle + b)$. Note that this is very similar to regularized logistic regression, which uses the term $1/(1+\exp(-y_i(\langle w, x_i \rangle + b)))$ instead of $\max(0, 1 - y_i(\langle w, x_i \rangle + b)$, but with additional sparsity properties (only a subset of data points are active in the final solution) that make it more robust to outliers. The prediction accuracy was estimated via 5-fold cross validation. The regularization parameter was found to have little influence on the prediction accuracy, which is why it was set to the default value $C = 1$. We compared our SVM to the trivial baseline of a classifier that constantly predicts either -1 or 1; if the dropout probability in week i is denoted by p_i, then the classification accuracy of such a classifier is given by $\text{acc}_{trivial} := \max(p_i, 1 - p_i)$. The result of this experiment is shown in Figure 4. Note that we found it beneficial to use the "history" features, that is the information about the previous weeks only within the weeks 1–12. For the weeks 13–19 we switched the history features off (also the PCA above is computed without the history features). We observe from the figure that for weeks 1–8 we can not predict the dropout well, while then the prediction accuracy steadily increases. Our hypothesis here is that this could result from the more and more history features being available for the later weeks.

4 Conclusion

We proposed a machine learning framework for the prediction of dropout in Massive Open Online Courses solely from clickstream data. At the

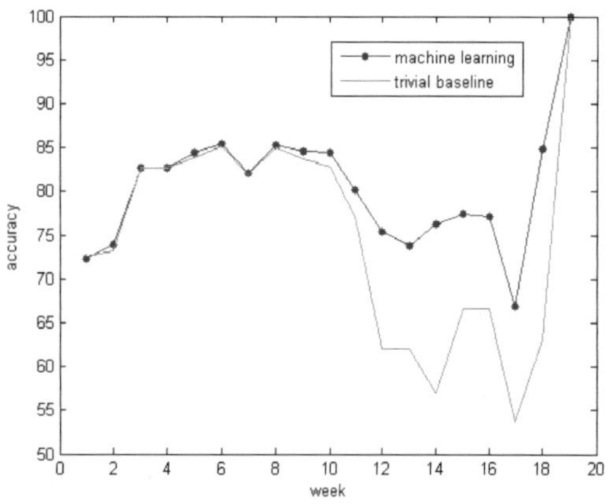

Figure 4: SVM classification accuracies per week. The baseline accuracy is computed as $\max(p_i, 1 - p_i)$, where p_i denotes the weekwise dropout probability.

heart of our approach lies the extraction of numerical features capturing the activity level of users (e.g., number of requests) as well technical features (e.g., number of screen pixels in the employed device/computer). We detected significant signals in the data and achieved an increase in prediction accuracy up to 15% for some weeks of the course. We found the prediction is better at the end of the course, while at the beginning we still detect rather weak signals. While this paper focuses on clickstream data, the approach could in principle also combined with forum data (e.g., using multiple kernel learning (Kloft et al., 2011)), which we would like to tackle in future work. Furthermore, another interesting direction is to explore non-scalar features (e.g., country, OS, browser, etc.) and non-linear support vector machines.

References

Katy Jordan. *MOOC Completion Rates: The Data.* Availabe at: http://www.katyjordan.com/MOOCproject.html. [Accessed: 27/08/2014].

Miaomiao Wen, Diyi Yang and Carolyn P. Rose. *Linguistic Reflections of Student Engagement in Massive Open Online Courses.* ICWSM'14, 2014.

Carolyn Rose and George Siemens. *Shared Task on Prediction of Dropout Over Time in Massively Open Online Courses.* Proceedings of the 2014 Empirical Methods in Natural Language Processing Workshop on Modeling Large Scale Social Interaction in Massively Open Online Courses, Qatar, October 2014.

Jason A. Brotherton and Gregory D. Abowd. *Lessons learned from eClass: Assessing automated capture and access in the classroom.* ACM Transactions on Computer-Human Interaction, Vol. 11, No. 2, pp. 121–155, June 2004.

C. Cortes and V. Vapnik. Support-vector networks. *Machine learning*, 20(3):273–297, 1995.

R.-E. Fan, K.-W. Chang, C.-J. Hsieh, X.-R. Wang, and C.-J. Lin. LIBLINEAR: A library for large linear classification. *Journal of Machine Learning Research (JMLR)*, 9:1871–1874, 2008.

M. Kloft, U. Brefeld, S. Sonnenburg, and A. Zien. ℓ_p-norm multiple kernel learning. *Journal of Machine Learning Research*, 12:953–997, Mar 2011.

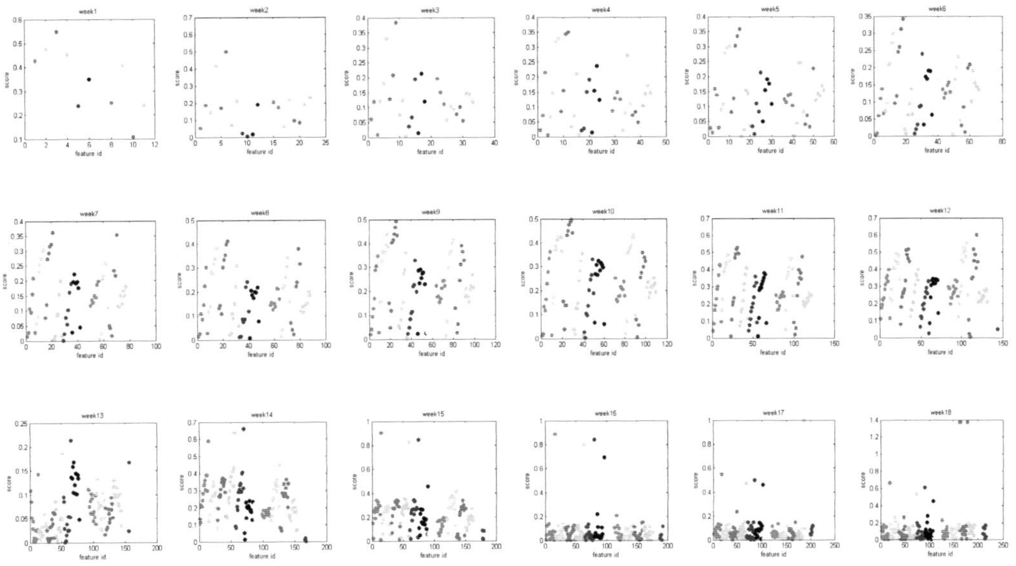

Figure 2: Fisher scores indicate which features are predictive of the dropout. Features are ordered from left to right with increasing ids; i.e., pink indicates the number of requests (feature id 1), cyan the number of sessions (feature id 2), etc. In particular, we observe that features related to a more balanced behaviour pattern such as the number of active days (feature id 3) are the most important ones in the first couple of weeks while more general features like the number of requests rise in importance past week 12.

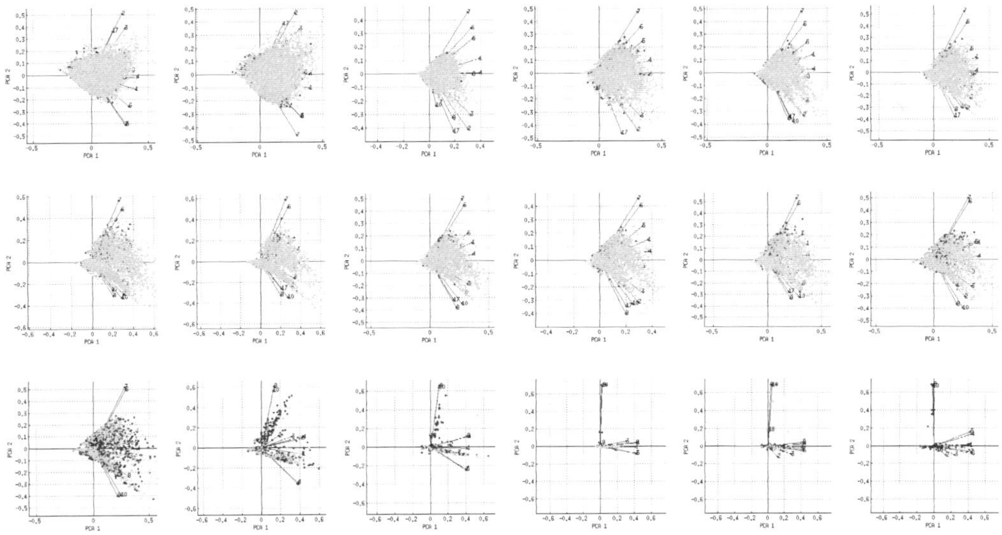

Figure 3: Result of principal component analysis. The data becomes more non-isotropic within the later weeks (from week 13), and can also be separated better.

Author Index